International Business for A2

2nd Edition

Alan Hewison & Nancy Wall

Alan Hewison is an experienced enthusiast for the joint subject approach. He is Head of Economics, Business and Politics at Queen Elizabeth Grammar School, Penrith, Cumbria. He is very experienced in curriculum development and has been a senior examiner for many years.

Nancy Wall was a teacher for the first half of her career. Since 1991 she has worked in curriculum development with a particular interest in teaching strategies and classroom resource development. She is an experienced author and editor and contributes to a wide range of publications and web sites.

Edited by Nancy Wall

© Anforme Ltd 2013
ISBN 978-1-905504-99-2
Images supplied by Shutterstock.com

Anforme Ltd, Stocksfield Hall, Stocksfield, Northumberland NE43 7TN.

Typeset by George Wishart & Associates, Whitley Bay.
Printed by Potts Print (UK) Ltd.

Contents

Using this book

Most users of this book will have studied one of two Edexcel courses, either AS Business Studies or AS Economics and Business. You will need to carry all that you learnt in the AS course along in your mind as a foundation for further work at A2. In particular, you will need to recall the definitions of key terms that are part of the AS courses and are not always repeated in this book.

Some of the chapters in this book provide background knowledge that will help you to understand the key elements of unit 3. The Introduction provides background on trade generally while Chapters 4-7 give you a basic understanding of the EU, China, India and other fast developing countries. The final chapter links what you have learnt to some of the very dramatic current events that are currently creating many uncertainties.

As far as possible the chapters relate closely to the course specifications. However this means that some topics require repetition. There are cross-references to other chapters to help you build your understanding of the course. As you proceed through the course, more and more of the threads in earlier chapters are picked up. We hope that this will help you to develop an overview of current trends and a strong understanding of key points.

Many specific businesses figure in the case studies but you should investigate other businesses as well, to get as broad a view as possible.

The questions relating to the case studies in this book are designed to help you to understand and to learn. They are not exam style questions and they will not help you to improve your exam technique. The Edexcel website has a wide range of past paper questions together with examiners' comments. You should practice these and read the comments to get feedback on your own efforts.

The link between trade and growth

Trade is a good thing

5000 years ago, there was a stone age axe factory on the side of a mountain, Pike o' Stickle, in Cumbria. The stone there was geologically unusual and made high quality axes. So when these axes turned up in several different places, it told us something about trade in the stone age.

Many axes from this area have been dug up in Lincolnshire and the East Midlands. But although most of the finds come from these areas, others have come from the Thames valley, Aberdeen, Ireland and numerous places in between. Now, these axe heads were made of stone and were heavy to carry. Evidence is accumulating that there was a route system, with markers and guides. You can see straight away that these apparently primitive people would have had to be highly organised to move such heavy products around.

Obviously some people benefited greatly from trade – if they hadn't they would have had no incentive to go to all this trouble. They probably used pack animals, but the axes were clearly valuable and they would have needed security during transport. Each axe must have commanded a high price – though it is hard to say what form payment took.

Questions

1. Which of the internationally traded products you buy are the most valuable to you?

2. List five such products that are important to you personally. For each one, work out why you didn't buy a substitute produced in the UK.

Trade has expanded steadily. The Romans bought silks from the Chinese. Medieval Europeans bought spices from India. The sailors who explored the world in the 15th and 16th centuries were interested in spices but the real motivation was the search for sources of gold. (Did you know that one consequence of Spain's opening up of the Americas was a big increase in world gold stocks and a burst of inflation?)

Colonisation was preceded by the opening up of trade routes. Minerals were important but so were furs from North America. Tea and coffee followed. All the people who got involved in these trends knew that trade makes you better off, for some, spectacularly so. (An irrelevant fact: the coffee shops in 18th century London were the forerunners of today's financial institutions in the City.)

Britain was fortunate. Technical advances in the 18th century led to the Industrial Revolution, which made it possible to export manufactures in exchange for raw materials and luxuries.

Life without trade is quite hard to imagine. You get to consume some goods and services that can't be produced locally. With imports we get more choices. But much trade between modern economies is about competition on price and quality. For exporters it is all about finding new and bigger markets which will lead to growing profits.

Figure 1 (page 2) shows the link between exports and economic growth since 1950. You can see that economic growth rates fluctuate, but exports are much more volatile. The picture is one of rapid change, at times quite painful, but overall having a big impact on incomes.

Structural change

Trade doesn't just make you better off. It changes what economies produce. Resources move into profitable lines of production. Some businesses grow and some shrink (although those facing falling demand can diversify successfully if they are nimble enough). This is structural change. It is good for consumers who

are choosing the products they prefer, but not so good for people who work in the declining sectors, or for those with capital invested in them. They do protest when it happens, and they put pressure on governments to do something. Then it becomes difficult for governments to distinguish between the impact of trade on standards of living generally, and the loss of livelihood that occurs when demand for individual products falls significantly. Usually the majority of the population are benefiting from rising incomes while a minority are having problems because they are associated with declining industries.

Figure 1: Growth in volume of world merchandise exports and GDP, 1950-2011

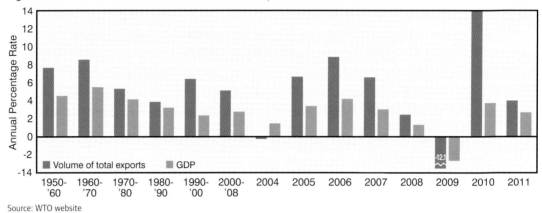

Source: WTO website

Shocks

Economies experience shocks, inevitably. Some are natural – like the Asian tsunami in 2004. That was devastating for local economies and very difficult for the countries affected. Other shocks are man-made.

● Steep increases in oil prices in 1974 and 1980 caused people to spend so much more on energy consumption that recessions followed, while producers of everything else faced greatly reduced sales. Eventually the oil exporters began to buy more of the importing countries' exports and oil prices first stabilised and then fell (in real terms). Recovery followed. In 2011-13, high petrol prices reduced motorists' spending power in already depressed economies. The effect was smaller than before but still very noticeable.

● Financial crashes in 1929 and 2008 led to greatly reduced spending and falling demand for many products.

● On a smaller scale, the reunification of Germany in 1989, followed by the liberalisation of all the east European economies, brought many new players into the international market place.

At times of change there is much pressure on governments to adjust their policies to help the losers – the people and institutions that face real trouble. The government reactions to the Great Depression in the 1930s created a learning experience, the importance of which is still very visible today. Many governments set up trade barriers, trying to save jobs at home by excluding imports. Some tried to devalue their currencies to make their exports more competitive, and to help their domestic producers to compete with imports. These became known as 'Beggar thy neighbour policies'.

The end result of these policies was to reduce international trade significantly. Trade diminished, more people lost their jobs and incomes fell further than they need have. Try asking your grandparents what happened to them or their parents in the 1930s. Most family histories include individuals who faced significant problems at that time.

After World War II

In the late 1930s rearmament brought the stimulus that the world economy needed. When the protagonists had finished slaughtering each other they sat down together and decided what to do. The consensus view was 'Never Again...'. The governments of the day collectively set up the United Nations as a political arena. For the world economy, in 1946, they planned three important organisations that would provide a framework for trade, growth and prosperity.

- The **World Bank** (IBRD, International Bank for Reconstruction and Development) was set up to fund reconstruction of war torn economies. In time it became a vehicle for encouraging development in the poorer economies of the Third World, where it is still a significant source of finance and policy advice (which is often controversial).

- The **IMF** (International Monetary Fund) is concerned with monetary stability in the world economy. Members contribute quota subscriptions. To start with, a system of fixed, stable exchange rates was set up. This evolved in the 1970s into the floating rate system we have today. The IMF still provides loans for countries with balance of payments deficits which are causing their currencies to depreciate very sharply. It gives copious advice to individual governments on economic policy, which is often controversial. It still provides a useful talking shop for national economic policy makers.

- The **World Trade Organisation** (WTO) actually didn't get off the ground in 1946; it proved too difficult to reach agreement. As an interim measure the GATT was set up (General Agreement on Tariffs and Trade). This was a small, poorly funded organisation. But still it managed to organise regular trade negotiations that led to import controls being steadily reduced. This helped many countries to find new export markets. In 1995 GATT was relaunched as the WTO, with more staff and funding, to continue the process of trade liberalisation.

Italy's crisis

In 2012-13, the Italian government faced big problems: recession meant rising unemployment, falling tax revenue and a ballooning public sector deficit. To combat this, the government opted for austerity measures: cuts in government spending. For many businesses, this meant falling demand, worsening the effects of recession. Many ordinary people protested. An election failed to produce a clear winner but the public verdict on austerity was clear.

The IMF recommended structural reforms to encourage competition. Proposals included:

- A more flexible labour market, e.g. letting employees do a range of different jobs so that they could be used more efficiently; letting wages fall in some sectors (especially professional services); giving employers more freedom to make people redundant.
- Strengthening competition law, e.g. by preventing price fixing.
- Encouraging more suppliers to compete in energy markets.
- Reducing barriers to entry (e.g. regulations that make it difficult to set up a new business).
- Privatising parts of the public sector so that individual businesses would compete.

In 2013, the IMF was still urging the new government to implement such reforms. Many people and vested interests opposed them. But the IMF view can sometimes encourage governments to persevere with unpopular but necessary policies.

Fast growing trade

Over the past few decades trade has grown spectacularly – as can be seen in Figure 1. Billions of jobs have been created and in China alone, it is said that 600 million people have been brought out of extreme poverty. What made this possible?

- **Trade liberalisation:** the international negotiations under the GATT and then the WTO were very long drawn-out, each round of talks taking many years to complete. But the process of reducing import taxes and cutting quota restrictions really did open up markets for exporters. Some countries benefited more than others but few failed altogether to get some rise in incomes. Those that did not benefit were mostly afflicted by wars and unrest.

- **Falling transport costs:** new technologies reduced transport costs across the board. Containerisation both cut costs and made transport more flexible and controllable. Buying imports became cost effective for many more products than previously. Cheaper air travel and transport boosted tourism and made air freight realistic for many products. This not only increased consumer choice but also increased competition amongst producers, driving down the prices paid by consumers.

- **More trade blocs:** sometimes negotiating trade deals with a few neighbouring countries is much quicker and easier than global trade negotiations. The EU and NAFTA (the North American Free Trade Agreement) both helped businesses to sell their exports in other member countries.

- **More trade means more specialisation and greater efficiency:** specialising actually reduces input costs and prices, allowing business to reach larger markets with competitive products.

These trends are discussed in more detail in Chapters 2 and 14.

Interdependence

Specialisation is all about buying the best value product from wherever it is available. So buyers are often dependent on sourcing their requirements from other countries. But global interdependence is about capital, as well as consumer goods. Foreign direct investment (FDI), investing capital in other countries, has been highly significant in the development of new, competitive production facilities. The multinational corporations, sometimes called transnationals, the big businesses that are active in a number of different economies, have facilitated much of the growth of trade. Most of them see growth in their own turnover as an end in itself and a source of ever increasing profits. So they invest in the economies in which they have an interest, either as importers or exporters.

A natural consequence of interdependence is that change in one economy will affect many other economies. The government policies of trading nations will have an impact far beyond their own borders. So there is a great need for international co-operation. However imperfect the international organisations are (and they usually are even more imperfect than national organisations), we need them to facilitate international negotiations. Besides the ones already mentioned, the G8 and G20 have proved important since the financial crisis started in 2007.

Very significant quantities of imports come to the richer countries from poorer ones. Lower labour costs in the latter often make it possible to cut prices, or introduce new products (e.g. out of season vegetables and flowers). Before deciding that you won't buy these products, spare a thought for the people who produced them. When they got a job with an exporting business, they would have increased their incomes, often from a very low level.

Airbus and Boeing

Over the years, two big companies have emerged as major producers of civil aircraft. Boeing is the biggest aircraft manufacturer in the USA. Airbus is based at Toulouse in France, but is closely linked to Britain's BAe and to German and French aircraft manufacturers as well.

Both companies have huge research programmes and trade on their technical expertise. Sometimes one appears to be beating the other... until the other comes out on top for a time. Mostly in recent years, Airbus has actually delivered more planes.

So what happened when the Credit Crunch got under way in 2008? Well, orders dropped like a stone, for both companies. The gloomy outlook caused many travellers to stay at home and holiday nearby, or talk on the phone with their overseas business partners. Then as sales recovered, the euro fell, giving Airbus a competitive edge over Boeing. Yet in 2011, Boeing bounced back, selling more planes than Airbus, where profits sank. Then in 2012, the two were again running neck and neck.

Question

Collect the data for the US$/€ exchange rate, and orders and deliveries for Boeing and Airbus. (Wikipedia can help with this, although recent data may be estimated rather than real.) Is there news of customers switching to Boeing? Or can Airbus maintain its popularity?

Chapter 1

Why search for new markets?

Vodaphone

Telecomms are a fast growing sector but Vodaphone has never been less than vigorous in expanding its international operations. The data below shows how the company managed to grow, despite a world economy in recession. Even if you allow for the company blowing its own trumpet, the results look good, considering what was happening across the world economy. The percentages show like-for-like growth, excluding the effect of inorganic growth, i.e. company takeovers or new acquisitions.

Table 1.1: Vodaphone's performance

		2010	2011	2012
Service revenue; % organic growth	The main measure of group sales	£44.5bn -1.6%	£45.9bn 2.1%	£46.4bn 1.5%
Operating profit (related to organic growth)	Main measure of operating performance	£11.5bn	£11.8bn	£11.5bn

Source: Company Accounts, 2012

Much of Vodaphone's growth has come from activities abroad.

- At the start of operations in India in 2007, sales revenue there was £28 million; by 2012, it was £150 million. At first, Vodaphone's prices were not competitive but then it introduced low-cost handsets; market share rose from 16% to 21%. In the year to March 2012, Vodaphone's revenue from India grew by 19%.

- In 2011, 140 million people in India acquired mobile phones.

- M-Pesa, Vodaphone's money transfer facility, processes £600 million every month. This attracts a huge number of customers who do not have access to bank accounts.

- By 2013, it was clear that sales revenue was falling. But profits remained at the same level as in previous years. Energetic cost cutting and concentrating on the growth areas – data services and emerging markets – had made the business leaner and fitter. 70% of mobile users are in emerging markets.

Source: Industry data

The chairman's statement said:

> Our focus on the key growth areas of data, emerging markets and enterprise is positioning us well in a difficult operating environment. Our goal over the next three years is to continue to strengthen our data networks and to enrich customers' experience.

Discussion points

1. Why is Vodaphone concentrating on expansion abroad?

2. Given the growth of mobile phone usage in India, evaluate Vodaphone's performance.

3. Why might sales revenue have grown more slowly in 2013?

4. What might Vodaphone do to retain its competitive edge in the future?

Reasons for trading internationally

In 2008, Vodaphone was the biggest UK mobile operator with 25% of the market. The other three big players were O2 with just slightly fewer than Vodaphone, T-Mobile with 23% and Orange with 21%. Then in 2010, T-Mobile and Orange agreed to merge while retaining their individual brands. Between them they had a staggering 43% of the UK market, with 29.5 million subscribers. The merger was cleared by the EU competition authorities and by the UK's Office of Fair Trading (OFT).

It would be hard for Vodaphone to expand its **market share** in the UK. There is no point in thinking that the market for mobile phones will expand rapidly. As in most developed countries, the number of mobiles is now greater than the population, with 130 subscriptions per 100 of population. Growth will be modest. The growth of mobile phone usage is actually most spectacular in the poorest countries where the infrastructure for land lines, outside big cities, barely exists. Market penetration in Africa reached 80% in 2013. Africa has passed China and India – where land lines are more readily available.

> **Market share** is the percentage of total sales of one particular product that comes from an individual business.

Figure 1.1: Mobile phone users by market, 2011

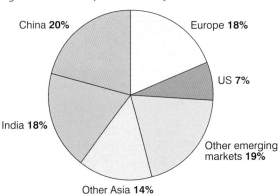

China **20%**   Europe **18%**

US **7%**

India **18%**

Other emerging markets **19%**

Other Asia **14%**

Source: Company Accounts, 2012

Mobile subscriptions have reached the point of **market saturation** in developed countries. People will replace their handsets but subscriptions will rise very slowly from now onwards. Meanwhile the growth of the markets in emerging economies has been spectacular and for a while this will continue. It is no surprise therefore to find that the big multinational mobile operators have moved into the countries where they can expand their markets.

Market penetration can be measured using the number of subscriptions per 100 people. In the UK in 2002 this was 75%. By 2007 it was 111%, and by 2013, 130%. The emerging markets are not far behind: market penetration worldwide reached 86% in 2013 and was still going up by 17% each year. The data is not always consistent and easy to compare, but the overall picture is clear enough – there has been a market bonanza for the mobile operators. Of course, they haven't had it all their own way. Local operators compete with the multinationals and that limits the earnings of the latter in emerging markets. Vodaphone has had to make big price cuts to compete with local operators in India.

> **Market saturation** occurs when it becomes impossible to expand sales further in that particular market. If the product is a durable good, e.g. a washing machine, it may still be possible to sell replacement machines.
>
> **Market penetration** refers to the process of expanding market share so as to reach a larger number of customers.

Mobile subscriptions have reached the point of market saturation in developed countries.

What are the limits in the domestic markets?

The mobile market is exceptionally dynamic. But on a more modest level, similar conditions apply to many businesses. Competition from other producers can create a tough trading environment. Governments in developed countries want to encourage competition. In the UK, the OFT works to prevent individual businesses from acquiring too much market power. Competition policy keeps prices down for consumers and it gives businesses an incentive to produce efficiently. So businesses find that they cannot easily expand their market share in their domestic markets.

Tesco provides a good example: one pound in every nine spent by consumers in the UK is spent at Tesco stores. That gives the company a truly amazing level of market penetration. Sure enough, Tesco has had trouble with the competition authorities, which have dictated rules about where and when Tesco has too many outlets for customers to have a real choice. These rules limit Tesco's capacity to open new stores. So now there are over a hundred Tesco stores in Japan and in Thailand and outlets all over Eastern Europe, especially in Poland. Tesco also has a strong presence in many other countries. Its venture into the USA was not a success. But never mind, the company is now truly multinational and risks in any one country can be set against successes in others.

For some businesses, the constraint is coming from competing imports. Businesses can react vigorously, cutting costs and increasing productivity or improving product design. But ultimately if the foreign competitor has a significant market share, the domestic producer may face real difficulty in expanding. Exporting may be the only way to achieve higher sales.

A relatively small domestic market may provide insufficient sales revenue to make expensive innovations worth the cost of research and development. Global reach is important here because the prospect of sales in foreign markets greatly increases the expected future income stream from any proposed innovation. Of course there are risks. Development costs may overrun. How could Airbus possibly have contemplated developing the A380, its newest wide-bodied airliner, if it did not have a global market? There were interminable glitches in the development process – there usually are, with new aircraft. These pushed up the cost. But the advance orders from Singapore Airlines and others provided the incentive to carry on.

> **Innovation** may mean either a new product development or an improvement in the design of an existing product. Both of these are product innovations. Alternatively, process innovation means cutting costs by finding a better method of producing.

Some products are constantly being superseded by technical changes and innovations. This always happens with machines and electrical goods – cars, washing machines, computers and so on. Suppliers have to keep abreast of new technologies, patent their own discoveries and innovate as fast as they can, just to stay in business. An international market increases the incentives to keep on researching potential innovations and reduces the risks. Sales may drop off in one market but are less likely to diminish in all markets at once. Competing companies will be innovating too, and maintaining competitiveness means keeping up and if possible surpassing the achievements of rival businesses.

Extending the product life cycle

Very often, businesses have to work hard just to keep the market share they have. Staying competitive in a stable market is one thing, but supposing the product has passed through the growth and maturity phases of the product life cycle and is going into decline. What do you do next?

> The **product life cycle** refers to the phases which many products go through between their first introduction to the market and the eventual decline in sales that may lead to production ceasing. These phases include development, introduction to the market, growth, maturity (during which sales are fairly constant) and decline. (Go back to unit 2 if you have forgotten the details.)

The length of the product life cycle varies hugely from one product to another. Cadbury's Dairy Milk is famous for having lasted more than 100 years, as have Kelloggs Corn Flakes. In contrast, vinyl LPs lasted about 30 years, until they were superseded by CDs. Technical change is always going to be important in bringing a product to the end of its life but changes in fashions and tastes also can bring about a very rapid decline in sales.

Extending the product life cycle can work. Improvements and subtle changes in the product may help it to keep its market. But if tastes or fashions are involved, the decline phase of the product life cycle may be surprisingly swift. New markets may provide sales growth that would be impossible to achieve in the domestic market through minor product changes.

Charles Tyrwhitt's shirts

The city's favourite shirtmaker, Charles Tyrwhitt, is continuing its global expansion. Unfazed by the recession, the founder, Nick Wheeler, is going forward with his plan to become the world's leading shirtmaker. Not satisfied with having stores in London, Manchester, New York, Madrid, Paris, Singapore and Kuwait, Charles Tyrwhitt is now exploring the Indian market.

The company is working with the Collective Store in India's fashion capital, Mumbai, launching their shirts as a super premium lifestyle retail brand 'for the discerning man'. The Collective is the anchor store at the Palladium, the city's first high-end luxury brands mall.

Charles Tyrwhitt sells to over 77 countries worldwide and has a turnover of £60 million per annum. The firm has recently made huge in-roads into the German market, which is up 52% year-on-year exclusively through mail order and internet sales. Now, they are hoping to win over Indian businessmen with their premium quality shirts.

Nick Wheeler says, "we are delighted to be part of The Collective Store. Their position as an upmarket, high-quality outlet goes perfectly with our target audience and has helped us to position ourselves in the Indian market." Recently, Tyrwhitt's annual average profit growth has been over 50%.

Source: company press releases.

City types wear traditional shirts and like the wide variety of colours and designs that Charles Tyrwhitt offers. But fashion conscious customers are very fickle indeed and there is always a risk with fashion items that the bottom will drop out of the market. Associating the product with Britishness and exporting it makes sense as a way of reducing the risk of fashion changes. It also taps into similar market segments in other locations, giving potential for widening the market.

Exporting services

You might think that most UK exports would be manufactured but in fact trade in services is important too. Accountancy and insurance both offer many opportunities for UK businesses. Tourism is another obvious service that can generate revenue for a wide range of businesses, and of course financial services have been a big money spinner in the past. Financial service exports could yet be affected by future banking regulations or difficulties in the relationship with the EU. But service exports are sure to remain important to the UK – they are usually around 40% of total exports.

Business objectives

The search for new markets has different features for each product and location. The underlying reasons for it will always have roots in the desire to expand the business, make more profit and spread the risks associated with growth. Bigger businesses can take some risks without threatening their futures. New markets mean sales growth and profits that will fund further expansion. The entrepreneur may sleep a little easier and gain great satisfaction from an expanding marketplace.

Chapter 2

Why have imports grown?

Dyson

Everyone knows about the bagless vacuum cleaner. It used to be made in Wiltshire, at the Dyson factory in Malmesbury. Once they hit the market, sales took off and in time James Dyson wanted to build a bigger factory. But he hit a serious problem with this idea: he could not get planning permission where he wanted it. He began to look further afield, specifically at locations where wage costs would be lower. The end of that story is that vacuum cleaner production moved to Malaysia in 2003.

Dyson kept the design, development, marketing, logistics and after-sales service functions in Malmesbury. He carried on innovating. He produced the high speed hand drier, which is very popular with users. Meanwhile the vacuum cleaners, the cash cow, a good source of profits, cost a little less to produce and continue to sell well.

So costs were down and profits were up. The company spends 12% of turnover on R&D. Employment at the Malmesbury premises is higher than it was when they were manufacturing there. They've recruited more scientists and researchers. Besides manufacturing in Malaysia, they are now producing in China and South Korea as well. Inevitably some employees in Malmesbury lost their jobs.

Sir James Dyson blames the City's obsession with high short term returns for his problems with manufacturing in Britain. His products involve a lot of investment ahead of their launch on the market. That said, production overseas has worked for this company.

Questions

1. What kinds of products can be outsourced in this way?

2. What potential problems may arise when companies outsource production?

3. What are the alternatives to outsourcing the whole production process?

4. What are the potential benefits for companies that outsource production?

When thinking about global sourcing it is helpful to look at the production process as a **supply chain**. This starts with the purchasing of the inputs, follows through the process of creating the product, moving the product to the point of sale and finalising the payment process. Inputs will come from a wide range of sources. For each input there will be alternatives. Starting with raw materials, they can usually be bought in from a range of possible suppliers. Components can be produced by the company, in-house, or they can be bought in from other businesses. The capital equipment and the labour needed in the production process can be part of the company. But equally, the production process can be contracted out to an independent business. This is known as **outsourcing**.

> **Supply chain:** the sequence of processes which starts with acquiring the most basic inputs and ends with delivery of the product to the customer.
>
> **Outsourcing** means buying necessary inputs from independent suppliers, either in the same country or overseas. It can apply to components, or complete products, or business services such as IT.

Different production locations can be used for each stage in the supply chain. It is sometimes possible for an entire manufacturing process to be located in one place but often, inputs will come from a range of locations. Costs of production will usually be different, depending on where production takes place. Supply chain managers decide where to buy each of the inputs and where to locate each element of the production process, comparing costs and lead times and considering quality issues. The objective is to optimise efficiency at every stage of the supply chain.

So whereas the businesses that figured in Chapter 1 globalised their activities by finding new markets for their products, others globalise their input sources or their production process. Sometimes they build their own factories abroad. Quite often, in order to do this, businesses will set up **joint ventures**. This is particularly likely in China, where foreign businesses need a partner to help them to get established in the Chinese economy.

> **Joint ventures** involve businesses in a collaborative relationship with a local producer. They are of particular value to businesses that want to produce and/or sell in an unfamiliar market. They can be used as a way to spread risks.

Alternatively, a business may sub-contract all of its production to independent businesses located in a country with lower costs of production (Nike does this). Supply chain managers will help businesses to find the lowest cost location for each stage of the production process. Where inputs are outsourced from overseas, the process is sometimes called offshoring or offshore outsourcing.

Global sourcing

A key question will always be, where can we find the lowest cost labour with the right skills and attitudes? This is not just a question of wage rates. The answer hinges also on levels of education and cultural characteristics. Dyson didn't at first go to China, where labour was still very cheap at the time. They went to Malaysia where wages were higher than in China, though less than in the UK. But in Malaysia they would find it easier to recruit people with the right skills and more people would be accustomed to speaking English in a business context. Also, the business would expect less difficulty in complying with local regulations.

Dyson were looking to manufacture a finished product in a single location. But many businesses either import certain inputs or locate just one or two stages of the production process overseas.

What are the benefits?

As with imports generally, there are benefits to be had when the imported items are unavailable in the domestic economy. So there are very obvious examples of imported inputs that are essential for the production process. These include raw materials such as copper and other minerals, some agricultural products e.g. pineapples, and a few manufactures that embody local skills that are not available in the UK, e.g. silk products. The importer may be a business that will use the inputs to produce the final product, or it may simply package and distribute what it has imported.

These types of imports are now just a small part of total trade. The big increase in imports that is part of the process of globalisation consists mainly of manufactures and services that could be bought on the domestic market but only at a higher price. We may buy Japanese electronic products because they are cheaper or better quality or more reliable, or some combination of these that makes them better value for money. These kinds of imports give us all more choices. They also encourage competition, so that consumers pay lower prices for all such products. This raises standards of living by giving consumers more purchasing power overall.

As well as importing finished products, businesses may simply buy standardised components that they can use in the process of assembling their finished product. (These are sometimes called semi-manufactures or intermediate products, terms that you may see in the official trade data.) The importing business is simply

buying its inputs from the supplier that offers the best value. There is a massive amount of trade in computer silicon chips for computers, many of which come from Intel. The company is based in California but much of its manufacturing activity takes place in Asian locations. The chips are then exported worldwide to customers engaged in manufacturing computers and computer-controlled products. Car manufacturers also often buy imported components, some of which come from relatively small businesses in the UK.

Airwell-Fedders

Since 1986 Fedders have made air conditioners in the USA. These were air conditioners for individual rooms, that fit into a window. In the nineties, the company realised that it was facing falling demand in a mature market. As far as individual air conditioning units were concerned, the market was saturated. New homes were being built with central air conditioning; owners of the individual units would replace them but the competition was stiff.

Fedders needed to reduce production costs and find a way to generate increasing sales. The Chinese market beckoned: summers there are very hot and many people in China still have no air conditioning at all. First the company hired twenty Chinese-speaking US citizens. They helped Fedders to find a joint venture partner, Ningbo General Air Conditioning Factory. They needed a partner because they would face stiff competition in the Chinese market. The two partners spent time establishing personal relationships so that a sense of trust could develop. Fedders needed the support of the regional government.

Then Fedders addressed design issues. In China, an air conditioner is still a major purchase for many people, and often a status symbol. Fedders needed to adapt their utilitarian designs to give them more sophistication.

What were the benefits? The Chinese partner got funds for investment and access to new technologies which would ultimately allow cost cuts. Fedders got a reliable source of low cost components for its factories in the US, and a chance to sell its air conditioners in the vast Chinese market. It got local expertise for sales, distribution and customer service.

In 2008 Fedders was acquired by a European company, Airwell, which is a big global supplier of air conditioners but especially strong in Europe and Africa. Fedders' production and distribution networks enable Airwell to expand world-wide. The combined operation no longer produces air conditioners in the US, although sales there are still significant. Production facilities are located in the EU, Israel, Argentina and China.

Questions

1. Why do you think the air conditioner factories in the USA closed down?
2. Assess the possible benefits for Fedders of the joint venture with Ningbo.
3. Assess the merits of Airwell's acquisition of Fedders.
4. Research a company that produces or distributes in a range of different countries. Find out why it developed its various activities and chose the locations that are important to it.

Outsourcing a specific process

There is nothing to stop businesses from continuing to base their production in their home location, but outsourcing particular processes. One UK manufacturer of high quality men's shoes wanted to continue producing in the UK but was fighting rising wage costs that could not be passed on by raising prices. So they looked at the most labour intensive part of the production process – stitching the leather uppers. They outsourced this to a Thai factory which had access to cheaper skilled labour. They were already getting an independent company to design their shoes and were comfortable with outsourcing. They were still able to control the quality of the product and claim with some justice that it was made in the UK. The cost savings were well above the extra transport costs.

Figure 2.1: Shoes in a supply chain

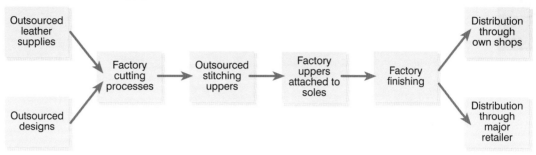

What made globalisation possible?

It has always been possible to import inputs. The UK was not particularly rich in natural resources at the time of the industrial revolution and initially many raw materials were imported (e.g. raw cotton for the textile industries).

Since WWII tariffs on manufactured goods have fallen steadily, thanks mainly to the General Agreement on Tariffs and Trade (GATT) and, latterly, the World Trade Organisation (WTO). This is known as **trade liberalisation**. The removal of many trade barriers, the creation and expansion of free trade blocs and the expansion of the WTO, particularly as exemplified by China's accession in 2001, has opened up the world to trade. China's share of world output increased from just over 2.6 percent in 1980 to 11.8% in 2011. China also joined ASEAN (Association of Southeast Asian Nations) creating the world's largest free trade area by population and third largest by GDP. All of these reductions in trade barriers on exports and imports have caused a tremendous increase in trade. Table 2.1 shows the change; there has been little further change since 2004.

> **Trade liberalisation** refers to the process of limiting and reducing barriers to trade so that economies ultimately move closer to free trade, meaning that there may be no trade impediments at all. International trade negotiations and agreements between WTO members have been the main ways to achieve this but regional trade agreements and trading blocs are also part of the story.

Table 2.1: Import duties as a percentage of the value of manufactured goods

	1913	1950	1990	2004
Germany	20	26	5.9	3.6
Japan	30	25	5.3	3.9
Italy	18	25	5.9	3.6
USA	44	14	4.8	4.0

Source: Globalisation and the changing UK economy, Department for Business, Enterprise and Regulatory Reform 2008

Communications and transport

There is a close relationship between the level of communications and the degree of globalisation. Advances in technology have made it much easier to organise and co-ordinate business operations around the world. The cost of telecommunications has fallen dramatically in recent years, thus encouraging trade. It is possible to conduct conference calls between several countries on mobile phones practically anywhere. Computers and broadband enable complex information to be passed easily and swiftly from one country to another. The new generation of fibre optics will speed this even further.

The humble shipping container has revolutionised global trade.

Businesses can make quick decisions, reacting swiftly to dynamic changes in markets and seizing opportunities ahead of the competition. Given good collaboration and management teamwork, businesses can set up complex and cost effective supply chains with a minimum of risk.

Table 2.2: Index of changes in transport and communications costs over the period 1930-2004

	1930	1950	1960	1970	1990	2004
Air transport cost per passenger mile	100	44	56	24	16	12
Cost of a 3 minute telephone call from London to New York	100	22	19	13	14	< 1
Cost of using a satellite	n/a	n/a	n/a	100	8	2

Source: Globalisation and the changing UK economy, Department for Business, Enterprise and Regulatory Reform 2008

Transport

Advances in transport and air travel have made it possible for business people to move much more easily around the planet. Previously time consuming and arduous journeys are now possible, making it much easier for businesses to reach and communicate easily with one another. It is not just people who need to move from place to place, but also objects:

- The humble shipping container has revolutionised global trade by dramatically cutting the costs of shipping goods and reducing transit times. The container made shipping cheap because it eliminated much of the labour intensive loading and unloading of cargoes. This changed the shape of the world economy. It suddenly became viable to move many more goods over greater distances than before. Shipping costs no longer sheltered producers whose advantage was proximity to the customers. Manufacturers could integrate once-isolated factories into networks, so that they could choose the cheapest location for making a particular item yet still shift production from one place to another as costs or exchange rates dictated.

- Air freight prices have fallen far enough for some perishable products to be exported. Some products with a high value in relation to their bulk also benefited. Speed reduces the amount of time for which transport must be financed – it helps to close the time gap between production and final sale. Automated freight handling at airports helped too.

- Computerised data handling made it easier and cheaper to keep track of goods in transit.

All of these developments cut the costs of international trade and facilitated **globalisation**. The way a single container can be used to take goods by road or rail to the docks, be lifted onto container ships by cranes, and carry on similarly at the other end until it reaches the final market, has changed trade dramatically. With containers, it takes far less time to load and unload at the dockside. The impact of containers is shown in Figure 2.2. But all aspects of improved communication and transport have played their parts.

Figure 2.2: World merchandise trade

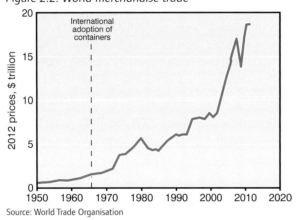

Source: World Trade Organisation

> **Globalisation** describes an ongoing process by which regional economies, societies, and cultures have become integrated through a globe-spanning network of communication and trade.

Containerisation

In 1961, before the container was in international use, ocean freight costs accounted for 12 percent of the value of US exports and 10 percent of the value of US imports. According to the staff of the Joint Economic Committee of Congress, "these costs are more significant in many cases than governmental trade barriers." At the time the average US import tariff was 7 percent.

Questions

1. Why would lower shipping costs speed the process of globalisation?

2. What effects do you think containerisation would have had on American producers and consumers?

All of these factors together meant that there were far more opportunities for trade generally. Retailers could shop around for interesting new products while exporters could realistically reach far wider markets. Producing in the lowest cost location meant that competition increased and prices fell, at least relatively. Outsourcing cut the cost of a huge range of manufactured products, because businesses could buy from the cheapest source.

This gave individual consumers more spending power – they could get what they wanted for less and so had funds left over to spend on other things. Possibilities for business expansion opened up all over the place. This is the story of globalisation – new export possibilities and cheaper imports.

Chapter 3

Global trade liberalisation

Buying clothes

How much of your income do you spend on clothes? See if you can work it out. It isn't all that important in your budget, is it? Not when you consider that the three basic needs are food, clothing and shelter. (Remember when you think about this to include the amount that parents or other relatives may have spent on your three basic needs recently.)

Until 2004, the international Multi Fibre Arrangement (MFA) put quotas on imports of clothing from each developing country that exported clothing, for each developed country. The quotas were fixed maximum quantities of each imported product and by making clothing scarcer, the MFA ensured that the prices to the consumer were higher than they would have been if trade had been free. Once the MFA ceased to operate, the prices of inexpensive clothing gradually fell.

Spending on clothing didn't rise much at all between 2000 and 2008; it was fairly stable at around £30 billion a year for the UK as a whole. But volume rose – spending the same amount, consumers got more for their money. Furthermore, that same pot of money was a declining percentage of their total incomes. Real incomes were rising on average by about 2.4% during that time period. The proportion of consumers' total incomes spent on clothing actually declined. We all had more to spend on other things, as well as more clothes. Maybe some of us ate more meals out or went a bit more often to the cinema.

Also during the period 2000-08 about a million new jobs were created in the UK. So removing the controls on clothing imported into the UK hasn't had any obvious effect on employment generally. What it has done is to create jobs in Bangladesh, where there are many factories making cheap and cheerful T-shirts and other items for the UK market. Bangladesh will be a little better off as a result and people there may buy more exports from the UK. Also, people in the UK who bought more meals out created more jobs in the UK, giving chefs a bit more purchasing power. Everybody gained. Trade is like that. Free trade is good for economic growth and raises incomes.

Questions

1. In your own words, explain how trade can raise incomes.

2. Look again at Figure 1 in the Introduction (page 2). What is the connection between exports and GDP?

3. Exports seem to be more volatile than GDP. Why might this be?

4. Meals out are just one product that might attract people who don't need to spend as much as they used to on clothing. Give three other examples of products for which demand might have increased as a result of clothing costing less.

International trade has increased dramatically over the past sixty years (see Figure 2.2 on page 15). In 1950, most of the world's manufactures were produced in the developed countries, i.e. those which had relatively high incomes, strong investment in capital equipment and the most advanced technologies. Developing countries, with low incomes and little capital, exported raw materials and agricultural products and imported manufactures. There was little trade in tourism.

In time, many countries were able to diversify their exports. Asian countries in particular developed manufacturing sectors while developed countries expanded trade in services. First Japan's exports grew dramatically and then in the 1970s, the Asian Tigers took off. (These were Hong Kong, Singapore, South Korea and Taiwan.) The Tigers are now seen as developed countries and are growing more slowly. The Bric countries – Brazil, Russia, India and China – are now seeing the massive increases in exports and GDP. This is having a huge impact because they are such large countries in terms both of population and geographical size. But they are not alone – many smaller countries are doing well too. These include Mexico, Indonesia and Malaysia but there are many others. Africa south of the Sahara is the only region which still depends largely on exports of primary products, though South Africa is emerging as a significant source of manufactures.

When exports are growing, GDP grows even more. The conditions that are favourable for economic growth are also favourable for the growth of trade. Rapid economic growth requires fast expanding markets. Countries that can export find that they can reap **economies of scale**, increasing their cost advantage and competitiveness.

> **Economies of scale:** as output grows, businesses can produce at lower average cost than before. They can usually then cut prices and enlarge their markets. Economies of scale come from a variety of sources: bigger machines that reduce unit costs (technical economies), cheaper loans (financial economies), more funds for research and development and specialist managers are all helpful possibilities.

As exports increase, developing countries earn foreign exchange and can use it to pay for imports. This creates larger markets for exporters in developed countries. In particular, the developing countries need capital equipment for their factories. But rising incomes will allow them to import some consumer goods as well. Trade is a two way process and there are benefits for exporters everywhere. The case study on page 16, on what happened as it became easier for developing countries to export clothing, has parallels in many other markets.

For many countries, the first manufacturing industries they could develop were textiles and clothing. They were able to compete with developed country producers because their labour costs were lower. As the new textile producers grew, they were able to use more sophisticated technologies and their prices fell further. Gradually, the economies where exports were growing strongly diversified into footwear, toys and other consumer goods. But they all knew that ultimately they would need to compete in hi-tech sectors as well. Even in the early 1990s, the Chinese government was investing in electronic products. To start with these were not competitive but they soon became much more so. The objective was to increase the value added in all lines of production.

To understand what made globalisation possible and how it developed over time, you really have to go back quite a long way and think through the events of the 1930s. Only then can you understand governments' commitment to trade liberalisation.

The Great Depression

After the 1929 financial crash, aggregate demand (the sum total of all demand in the economy) shrank so much that most export businesses, the world over, faced falling sales revenue. Then there were the businesses that sold on domestic markets but were in competition with imports. Their markets were shrinking too. Times were tough. Redundancies led to unemployment and great hardship. Governments tried to protect the stricken businesses, using import duties and other restrictions on trade. As more and more governments adopted this policy, international trade decreased further.

Some governments tried to devalue their currencies to make their producers more competitive. This would have worked for the first few that tried it. But then others followed suit until there were so many competitive devaluations that no country achieved anything except instability. Together, the trade restrictions and the competitive devaluations were called beggar-thy-neighbour policies.

(continued overleaf)

After World War II, many of the more powerful governments worked together to develop financial and trading rules that would prevent widespread use of these policies in the future, first through GATT and then WTO. From 1947 onwards there were long drawn out trade negotiations. Each 'round' of negotiations reduced import duties, and later on other kinds of trade restrictions were reduced too. Trade became steadily easier and more profitable. International trade grew – and then grew more. The vast majority of countries now belong to the WTO, believing membership to have many benefits.

Questions

1. Explain briefly in your own words why governments entered into trade negotiations to reduce import controls.

2. To what extent did the 1930s experience influence governments' reactions to the recession that followed the financial crisis of 2008?

How did this spectacular economic growth happen?

Economic growth has changed its nature. All through Victorian times, the UK economy grew by an average of 1% a year. Nowadays we would think this very slow. It wasn't steady growth either – there were ups and downs, booms and depressions. But living standards in 1900 were still a vast improvement on those of 1800. Other economies grew later but faster – as in the USA. The first economy to grow spectacularly, on the back of fast-rising exports, was Japan, during the 1950s and 60s. This pattern of economies growing fast while they catch up and then slowing down later is now widespread. (The Asian Tigers provide useful recent examples.)

Growth on this scale happens when all of the important component influences are at work.

- There must be **investment** in new productive capacity and also in **infrastructure**. Without transport and communication facilities, increased output cannot be taken to its market. Investment in capital equipment increases **productivity** – the amount that can be produced with a given quantity of resources. The funds can come from the domestic economy or from abroad.

- New and better technologies may be needed. This may require investment in **human capital** as well – the skills and capabilities of the workforce.

- There must be a market for the output, i.e. a market in which businesses can compete on price and quality, with appropriate distribution facilities. Export markets can provide possibilities for rapid change, but trade restrictions need to be low enough to allow exports to grow.

Investment is spending now that will generate income in the future. It may entail building factories and buying machinery, other types of construction, research and development spending or education and training.

Infrastructure includes all transport and communication facilities as well as the provision of basic services such as energy and water supplies. Examples include telephone systems and ports, as well as roads, power stations and drains.

Productivity means output per unit of an input, usually labour but also capital. So a useful measure of productivity is output per hour worked. Labour productivity is increased by adding more and better capital equipment to the production process, or providing more training to employees, or managing the workforce more efficiently.

Human capital refers to the knowledge and skills that people acquire through education, training and experience.

Some countries that have experienced export-led growth have had open economies. That means allowing importers to bring in goods with a minimum of restriction. Singapore is a good example. The government there saw free trade as a way of exploiting the strategic position of the economy – a south east Asian hub. Imports created a very competitive environment which forced businesses to cut costs. That made their exports competitive too.

Other economies have started out by restricting imports for a while, to give domestic industries time to get established. That can work but it means that labour costs need to be low to keep prices competitive. In time, governments want wages to rise so that standards of living improve. At that point it pays them to reduce trade restrictions. That makes it easier for fast growing firms to import new capital equipment and increase productivity. At the same time it encourages businesses to compete by being efficient rather than by paying low wages. China is at this stage now.

Globalisation

This process has provided some impetus to the WTO negotiations that have led to trade liberalisation. The more trade restrictions are reduced, the easier it is to export and the greater the scope for increasing incomes. These are not, however, the only forces at work in the globalisation process.

- International capital movements have played a big part in providing the finance for investment at every level. **Foreign direct investment** allows both new activities and relocation of existing production.

- **Trading blocs** – such as the EU – have created large markets within which trade is easier for member countries.

> **Foreign direct investment** (FDI) occurs when businesses set up factories or other kinds of production or distribution facilities in other countries. Much FDI flows from one developed country to another but increasingly, FDI is flowing into developing countries. It may be associated with outsourcing of production in countries with lower input costs, or it may be directed towards production for foreign markets.
>
> **Trading blocs** may be loose groupings of countries that want to trade without restriction, as with NAFTA, the North American Free Trade Association. The objective is free trade between Canada, Mexico and the USA. Alternatively a trading bloc may aim to create a common market, as has the EU. This aims to create a level playing field so that in addition to free trade, all regulations are harmonised and members combine to form a single market.

The role of FDI

Most governments welcome FDI. It creates jobs, sometimes in regions which badly need them. If the objective is to be close to the market, it may reduce imports. If it is to export, then the new activities will serve a wider market. The UK government facilitated the FDI that came with Nissan and Toyota manufacturing in the UK. The main motive for the two Japanese companies was to produce inside the EU, thus avoiding import duties.

Some FDI causes problems and these are explored in more detail in Chapter 18. Table 3.1 shows which economies are likely to benefit from it and which not. Economies which are in the very early stages of economic development are usually not attractive to foreign investors. They are more likely to be successful in attracting foreign aid payments from both governments and international organisations such as the World Bank.

Obviously, the significance of FDI depends in part on the population of the country concerned. US$1.3 billion is significant for Botswana with a population of 1.3 million, US$1.5 billion for the Congo is tiny, given its population of 68 million. War-torn or politically unstable countries are not going to attract much FDI until the prospects of profit are more visible.

Table 3.1: FDI destinations, selected economies, 2011

High inflows	US$ bn	BRICs	US$ bn	Low inflows	US$ bn
USA	257.5	China PRC	220.1	Mongolia	4.7
Belgium	102.0	Brazil	71.5	Congo (Dem.Rep.)	1.6
Hong Kong	95.4	Russia	52.9	Uzbekistan	1.4
France	45.2	India	32.2	Sri Lanka	1.0
Canada	39.5			Uganda	0.8
Germany	39.1			Botswana	0.6
UK	36.2			Macedonia	0.5
Spain	31.4			Paraguay	0.4
Italy	28.0			Laos	0.3
Netherlands	13.9			Mali	0.2

Source: World Bank

Notice that China, Russia and Brazil have had more FDI than India. This is not an accident. In the past, the Indian government never looked to increase foreign investment, preferring to rely on its own internal resources. This was a political decision, based on a sceptical attitude towards the possible benefits of welcoming multinational companies (MNCs). This is now changing, but slowly. In contrast, China has sought joint ventures with MNCs, as a quick way to develop export potential and acquire new skills and technologies. These policies might change over time.

Capital movements are an important feature of the globalisation process. As much as trade, they have hastened the development of economically interdependent relationships between countries. Access to foreign capital markets can greatly enhance the chances of setting up a new business successfully. Partnerships and joint ventures can do much to help inexperienced exporters in finding both finance and markets. FDI flows do change considerably from year to year.

Globalisation and growth do bring costs

There are two major sources of difficulty with globalisation. When trade patterns change, there are losers. In each economy, some businesses grow and some find that their markets are shrinking. Some industries decline. The UK has seen textiles, shipbuilding and iron and steel decline dramatically. Services have done well. Many young people come to the UK to study and the fees they pay are substantial. The financial sector is a big exporter. Trade involves **structural change**.

The other difficulty comes from the environmental degradation that usually accompanies rapid growth. The **external costs** of increasing output are often not paid for by the consumer. This leads to overproduction – more is produced and sold than would be if the price reflected the true costs of production. This is particularly likely when environmental regulations are lax, as they often are in developing countries. They cannot always afford expensive precautions against pollution and they are desperate to increase the incomes of poorer people. This is a continuing problem.

> **Structural change** occurs when some industries are declining while others are growing. Resources will move out of one line of production and into another. Some people will be made redundant. If they are able to retrain or relocate they will find it easier to get another job.
>
> **External costs** occur when production involves the use or degradation of resources which neither producers nor consumers pay for. Pollution and congestion are external costs.

Regulations which prevent businesses from creating external costs will increase the internal costs of production, as when investment in new equipment is needed to clean up emissions. Producers may have to raise prices to cover the extra costs and this can make them less competitive. Where there is intense global competition this gives an advantage to the dirtiest producers, and people who live nearby will suffer. Not all businesses rush to do something about external costs; most try to avoid doing anything for as long as possible. This tension underlies the difficult negotiations that bedevil attempts to introduce international agreements that might reduce unsustainable growth and the risk of climate change.

Similarly the price of globalisation is often paid by those who lose their jobs and have difficulty in finding new ones. While much of the world is enjoying rising incomes, the individuals who are without work may experience serious loss of income. Some countries do more to provide unemployment benefits than others. Where little or no unemployment benefit is available there is real hardship when structural change is taking place. Though the benefits to the many are great, robust welfare provision is needed to compensate the losers. Without such provision, structural change can have serious political consequences.

Globalisation, 2008-13

The financial crisis 2007-8 created a pause in the process of globalisation. You can see the overall effect on developing countries in Figure 3.1.

● Most developed countries experienced recessions and some faced rapidly falling incomes.

● Most developing and emerging economies held up fairly well. Sales in most of their developed country markets fell but they made up for that with increasing sales to each other. But by 2012 there were signs of slowing economic growth in many countries – notably in China.

● Rapid growth in a fast developing economy does not usually last for more than 30 years or so. That is the catch up period; when per capita GDP is getting to the point where the country is regarded as developed, growth rates will be similar to those of other developed countries. (S. Korea and Singapore provide good examples of this; earlier, from the 1980s, Japan slowed down too.)

> It is really difficult to guess how globalisation will develop over the next few years. Over to you! If you are reading this in 2014 or later, find out for yourselves. Reading this chapter, you have learnt something about how the globalisation took shape, before the instability of the years 2008-13. Chapter 20 looks at current issues in more detail.

Figure 3.1: Developing economies' share and growth rates of goods and services exports, 2005-2012

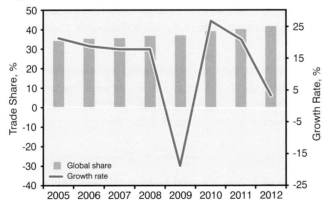

Source: UNCTAD

Chapter 4

The European Union

Specialising

Globalisation means that an individual business or a specific location can become very specialised in particular products. Take the machines that are used to make blister packs for pharmaceutical products. The pills go in at one end, little rubber suckers catch them in batches and drop them into plastic trays, then seal them in with foil. Inventing those machines took some clever engineering.

So where do the Big Pharma companies and the smaller scale producers of food supplements go for their packaging machines? For EU buyers, the chances are that they will go to one of three producers in Bologna, Italy. They could go to Minnesota, USA, or Quebec in Canada, where there are a few more producers. But the Italians are highly competitive within the EU and export to many countries. Why look further?

So you think the UK needs its own blister packaging machines? Sepha, in Belfast, manufactures them but specialises in machines for research and clinical trials. Clusters of manufacturers are still growing in Italy, Minnesota and Quebec.

Questions

1. UK trade with EU member countries has grown faster than trade with the rest of the world, since the UK joined the EU in 1971. Why might this be?

2. Evaluate the impact that the enlargement of the EU in 2004 had on UK businesses.

Trading blocs are becoming increasingly important in the global economy. The benefits of collaborating with neighbouring trading partners are becoming clearer in many countries. Trading blocs encourage specialisation and open up new markets. The businesses that are the most competitive can grow faster. This is what happened to the businesses that specialise in manufacturing packaging machines in Bologna. It means that there will be economies of scale and the costs and prices of some products will fall as a result. This in turn gives consumers greater purchasing power and higher standards of living.

All trading blocs are not alike. They fall into two broad groups – the **free trade areas** and **common markets**.

Free trade areas are groups of countries that trade completely freely with each other, with no trade barriers, but each member country retains its own independent trade policies in relation to the rest of the world.

Common markets have completely free trade internally and a single unified trade policy covering all member countries' trade with the rest of the world. But besides free movement of goods and services, there is also free movement of people and capital. Individuals in all member countries can work in any other member country. Businesses based within the common market can invest in any member country.

NAFTA, the North American Free Trade Area is a good example of a free trade area. It comprises Canada, the USA and Mexico. Some Americans have their doubts about it but it has opened up new markets for many businesses. Consumers in Canada and the US have had the benefit of highly competitive imports from Mexico. NAFTA has created jobs in all three countries.

The European Union is a common market. In fact it is now one massive **single market**. It has just on 500 million consumers and there is no doubt at all that it has increased trade between its members. There are now very few barriers to trading goods remaining within the EU. The overall objective of the EU was always to achieve faster economic growth. Many people looked to achieve political integration as well as economic integration, but for many reasons this has proved to be elusive.

The move towards the single market began in the late 1980s and was supposed to be complete by 1992. In fact it turned out to be an ongoing process. The idea was to create a level playing field, so that competing businesses would face similar requirements wherever production is located, and wherever they were selling their products, within the EU. Another objective was to enable people to work, and businesses to invest, in any member country, wherever would be most profitable. Free movement of people involves recognising member countries' qualifications; free movement of capital requires that governments allow foreign direct investment both into and out of their economies.

> In the **single market**, barriers to the movement of goods, services, people and capital have gradually been reduced within the EU, making it more and more like a single economy.

EU history

The EU started life as the European Economic Community in 1957, with six member countries, Belgium, France, Germany, Italy, Luxembourg and the Netherlands. The UK joined in 1973, along with other countries then and later. In 2004 many eastern European countries joined. Croatia joined in 2013. Turkey is a candidate country, along with Macedonia, Iceland, Montenegro and Serbia.

Many new opportunities have been created by the development of the EU. Enlargement during and since 2004 made it possible for eastern European countries to grow faster. But it also opened up new markets for the original 15 members, including the UK. From the business point of view, it has also provided a choice of locations where lower cost labour will be readily available.

There have been changes in the way in which the EU is organised and attempts to make it more democratically accountable through creating its own political institutions. However, these are still much less influential than the European Commission, the administrative heart of the EU in Brussels.

Harmonisation and the single market

Harmonisation is important because it leads to most regulatory controls on businesses being common to all EU member countries. For example, labour laws that require employers to avoid endangering or exploiting their employees can raise production costs. But if all the competing businesses within the EU have to stick to the same rules, none of them are disadvantaged when competing with each other. Similarly, safety requirements for products are the same for all. Businesses can create a standardised product and sell it right across the EU, rather than having to make slightly different products to suit each national market. This level playing field makes possible long production runs and economies of scale.

All businesses in the EU have to abide by EU competition law, as well as the laws of their own country. This prevents unfair competition, especially market sharing agreements that allow certain businesses to get away with charging higher prices than they would if they were competing. This has had a significant effect on competition and has led to consumers being charged lower prices for better quality products. It may be one of the most important benefits of EU membership for consumers.

The single market involved the end of border controls on traded goods. This greatly reduced the amount of paperwork and the delays that used to occur at border crossings. There is no doubt that the single market approach has contributed to the integration of EU economies. However, harmonisation has not extended to the adoption of a unified tax and benefit system. It would be impossible to secure agreement within the EU on this, at least for now. So there are still very real differences between member countries as to tax rates and benefit levels. France and Germany pay higher unemployment benefits than the UK. This may mean that incentives to work are less strong in those countries and may in part explain their higher unemployment rates in recent years.

How does trade policy work?

The EU has a common external tariff (CET) which means that all member countries levy import duties on imports from the rest of the world at the same rates. The EU negotiates as a single entity in WTO negotiations. Import controls have been progressively reduced in line with WTO agreements. This has made worldwide trade in manufactures much easier, but has not so far had very much effect on trade in agricultural products.

Free trade within the EU creates fertile conditions for **trade creation**. Businesses have more choice as to where they buy their inputs and where they sell their products. A larger market means increased production and economies of scale, leading to lower prices. These will enlarge their markets further. In this way, trade is created.

The CET leads to another important feature of trading blocs – **trade diversion**. To the extent that tariffs make competing imports more expensive within the trading bloc, buyers will tend to buy more products made within the trading bloc and fewer imports from outside it. Trade will tend to be diverted, away from non-member countries. In the EU there has been relatively little trade diversion as far as manufactures are concerned. But different trading arrangements for agricultural products have most definitely reduced imports from non-EU food exporting countries.

The Common Agricultural Policy (CAP)

The CAP protects EU farmers from foreign competition to a very considerable degree. EU import controls on food products are high. For many food items, world prices are often below the prevailing EU price. This really upsets agricultural exporters outside the EU. It allows EU countries to keep substantial agricultural sectors and produce much of their own food – this is trade diversion. Chapter 13 examines the effects of trade policy in general.

> **Trade creation** occurs when there is an increase in the total amount of goods and services traded because of reduced trade restrictions within a trading bloc.
>
> **Trade diversion** occurs when a trading bloc reduces imports from non-member countries, enabling businesses within member countries to increase sales inside the trading bloc.

Policy making

The European Commission is responsible for implementing and administering EU policies. It has the power to initiate policy changes: it makes the proposals for new laws. These are then debated in the European Parliament, before being sent to the Council of Ministers, where cabinet ministers can put national points of view and make changes. This creates a number of opportunities for discussion and adaptation before the proposals become law. Once laws are enacted, disputes can be resolved by the European Court of Justice.

In 2009, under the terms of the Treaty of Lisbon, the Belgian prime minister, Herman van Rompuy became the first permanent President of the European Council. His term of office will end in late 2014. Baroness Ashcroft was appointed as EU Foreign Secretary. Neither official was well known in 2009. It was clear that member governments' leaders did not want competition from an already famous politician but both have been very active in the interests of the EU as a whole.

EU benefits

We have already seen that increasing trade flows are associated with higher levels of economic growth. For many years after joining the EU, UK trade with EU member countries increased, relative to trade with the rest of the world. This probably has to do with two important factors:

- Larger markets provide opportunities for potential exporters, opening up possible economies of scale.

- Increased competition provides incentives both to cut costs (enhancing productive efficiency) and to meet customer needs more effectively (allocative efficiency).

The European Commission has been particularly effective in pursuing firms that have engaged in anti-competitive practices. These include market sharing agreements and price fixing. For example, in late 2009, the office of the Competition Commissioner investigated the market for car repairs. It found that car manufacturers had tried to protect their own dealers and repairers from competition in a number of ways, including withholding vital technical information from independent car repairers. Measures are being implemented to prevent this kind of protection and increase competition. Tackling anti-competitive practices has led to price cuts and improved efficiency in many products, contributing to economic growth.

In 2010, when the car industry was struggling because of recession, the French government put together an aid package for Renault. The government proposed that aid should be made conditional on Renault siting its new plant in France. This is strictly against EU competition rules – governments cannot subsidise their own national companies in ways that would give them an unfair advantage over competing EU producers. The Competition Commissioner protested vigorously.

Constraints

Getting agreement between 28 governments can be difficult. Compromises have to be made and inevitably, not all governments like all aspects of EU policy. There are national rivalries and leaders jockey for position. There are issues surrounding the extent of democratic control over the European Commission.

The advent of the euro has moved the eurozone much closer to being a genuine single market.

There are still many barriers to free trade within the EU, particularly in the service sector. Individual member countries regulate their service sectors very tightly, often protecting them from competition. The President of the European Commission, José Manuel Barroso, has said: "That the… single market is not yet delivering growth and jobs at its full potential can in large part be put down to the successful defence of established interests to the detriment of society at large." Many member countries still do not want to encourage further integration within the EU economy.

Some people argue that the UK would be better off outside the EU. Norway and Switzerland do quite well outside. Norway, as a member of the European Economic Area, attends all EU meetings but has no voting rights. Both countries adhere to EU regulations. They live comfortably with the requirements of the EU. However, the UK is not a small country, as they are. The UK's leaving the EU would affect the rest of the EU, which would itself change in response. When the dust settled the UK could be much worse off, especially if political considerations are taken into account. It is impossible to decide to what extent Europe's political stability rests on EU institutions but it seems likely that collaboration within the EU has reduced areas of disagreement between members.

What difference does the euro make?

The advent of the euro has moved the eurozone much closer to being a genuine single market.

● With all prices quoted in euros, it is harder for businesses to raise prices above the competitive level and still sell their products; this is called price transparency.

● No foreign exchange deals are needed in order to trade, reducing transaction costs.

● Businesses can operate free from the uncertainty stemming from fluctuating exchange rates.

That said, for many people the loss of political sovereignty is a worry. Individual governments cannot have their own monetary policies and the interest rate that is appropriate for the eurozone as a whole may be inappropriate for an individual economy. There can be no exchange rate depreciation for economies that find themselves with yawning balance of payments deficits, due to being uncompetitive. There is no choice but to deflate with possible falls in real wages, until competitiveness is regained.

A euro crisis

Greece joined the eurozone without meeting all of the convergence criteria, partly because the government massaged the statistics on which the decision was based. The actual government and trade deficits became so large in early 2010 that the country was threatened with bankruptcy.

Greece was forced to pay high interest rates to cover its deficit – which of course made the deficit larger. Help came from Germany and the European Central Bank (ECB) but only on condition that Greece made savage cuts in government expenditure (known as austerity policies). These were extremely unpopular with the Greek people. Similar but less extreme situations developed in Ireland, Spain, Portugal and Italy. By the time Cyprus got into trouble the German voters were furious; effectively this limited the scope of the bail-out and meant that all Cypriot depositors with more than €100,000 in their banks lost the rest of their money. This may have undermined trust in the banking system.

Discussion point

What happened since this was written? Do you think that economic growth in the eurozone can pick up fast enough to save the countries concerned from a very prolonged recession?

So there is a loss of flexibility involved in the single currency. This is why there are convergence criteria, which have to be satisfied for each country applying to join the eurozone. These relate to fiscal policy and government borrowing (i.e. taxes and government expenditure); the objective was to ensure that individual economies would not have wildly different inflation rates.

Another trade bloc

ASEAN is the Association of South East Asian Nations. For many years the member countries have held regular meetings to share common concerns and facilitate trade. In 2010, an agreement between ASEAN and China came into being, creating a fully fledged trade bloc, the China-Asean Free Trade Area. Tariffs were eliminated on 90% of products. The total population of this group is 1.9 billion. But for now, the tariff reductions apply only to China and the six core ASEAN countries, Thailand, Malaysia, Singapore, Brunei, Indonesia and the Philippines. For the remaining four ASEAN members, Burma, Laos, Cambodia and Vietnam, the target date is 2015.

The governments concerned hope that their collective GDP will rise by $48 billion by 2020, over and above the growth that might have been expected under the old trading arrangements. China expects to benefit from cheaper commodity imports. Businesses in Indonesia, Thailand and the Philippines are nervous – they may suffer from fiercer competition with Chinese manufactures. But they do want to benefit from China's rapid economic growth. They may find new markets there.

There will certainly be changes in the structure of production as the member economies adjust. However, the member countries can register 'sensitive products'. For these, tariffs will continue perhaps up to and beyond 2020. They include some electronic products, motor vehicles and some chemicals.

ASEAN also has bilateral regional trade agreements with Japan, South Korea, India, Australia and New Zealand.

Questions

1. Why might it be reasonable for the member countries of the China-Asean Free Trade Area to expect increased GDP to result from this agreement?

2. What changes may take place in the economies of the member countries?

3. What might be the impact of the changes on (a) real wages and (b) profits?

4. To what extent would you expect the benefits of free trade to improve standards of living?

Chapter 5

What is the impact of growth in China and beyond?

China today

Sheer size defines China. If you cut out a map of China and place it on top of a map of Europe with the same scale, it would reach from the middle of the Sahara desert to the north of England. If you look at the distance from east to west, China would reach from the west coast of Ireland to the eastern end of the Black Sea. There are 1.3 billion people. But much of China is mountainous or desert, inhospitable for people.

The economic development of China has been patchy: the big cities along the coast have become mighty modern powerhouses, growing at breakneck speed. The interior has seen some development in places but there are still remote areas where little growth is possible. There are still about 300 million people in rural areas with very low standards of living.

Chairman Mao Zedong, who led the Communist revolution in 1949, died in 1976. This opened the way for his successor, Deng Xiaoping, to introduce reforms which would allow private enterprise and trade with the rest of the world. The big cities along the Chinese coast were well placed to export manufactures once economic liberalisation began. Shanghai, the biggest, now has a population of 24 million, and all the features of a modern city.

Opening Shanghai to foreign investment created opportunities for both foreign owned and local businesses. Migrant workers moved in from the countryside to take up the jobs that were being created. The same thing happened in Shenzhen in the south, which now has 10 million people. This city is only an hour's train ride from Hong Kong. Away back in the 1980s, businesses in Hong Kong started to make links with producers in Shenzhen because the very low labour costs made it a competitive place to locate production. Consultants from Hong Kong could teach the Chinese everything they needed to know about quality and technology.

Contrast the east coast with Gansu province in the interior. The Chinese still think of Gansu as a 'backward' place, although it too has changed greatly. Nevertheless there is serious rural poverty, with many families struggling to grow enough food on marginal land, with limited irrigation and little machinery. Despite the very fast rate at which new jobs have been created in the big cities, there are still many people in the countryside waiting for opportunities. They have limited education and health care facilities and their housing is basic. Many are living away from the main road system and cannot get their farm products to a market where prices might be attractive.

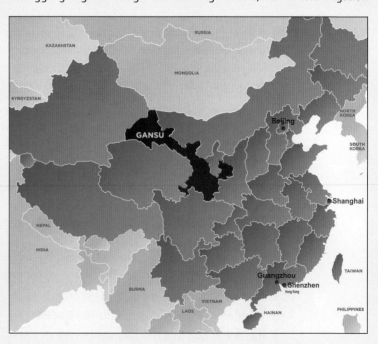

China continues to be governed by the Communist Party but the principles on which policies are based are pragmatic rather than Marxist. The party remains a powerful force in all aspects of economic life and all businesses must follow its requirements very carefully.

Questions

1. What might the Chinese government do to improve standards of living for poor people?

2. The Chinese government tries to limit the rate at which people migrate from the countryside to the cities. What disadvantages might this have?

3. Choose a Chinese industry – it could be electronics or toys or cars, but there are many others. Find out how it has grown and investigate its impact on standards of living and the environment.

Economic growth

When a relatively poor economy finds ways to develop, there follows a period of rapid catching up with high growth rates. Whereas rich developed countries may typically expect a long term trend rate of economic growth of around 2% per year, rates of 6-10% are common in countries that are developing fast.

These high growth rates appear to be sustainable for some years before they eventually slow down. You can already see this process working within China – Shanghai was growing at 8.2% per year in 2011, while the interior province of Chongqing (a big city in central China) was growing at a spectacular 14%.

Figure 5.1 shows economic growth rates for the BRIC countries, Brazil, Russia, India and China. These countries are not alone in growing fast but they are all very big economies. Chapter 7 looks in more detail at international comparisons.

Figure 5.1: Economic growth in the BRIC countries.

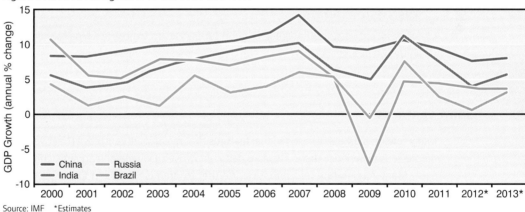

Source: IMF   *Estimates

China's rapid economic growth has made a real difference to the real incomes of most people. The Chinese are pleased with the progress that has been made and are anxious not to do anything that might impede further improvements. Early on in the liberalisation process, food production increased dramatically. Serious food shortages and malnutrition became a thing of the past. It is probably fair to say that everyone in China has experienced significant improvements in living standards since 1980.

Inequality

A key factor influencing standards of living is income distribution. Inequality means that a disproportionate share of national income is going to the rich, while large numbers of poor people remain poor. Table 5.1 shows the percentage of total income received by the poorest 20% of the population. A low figure implies

that the difference in income between the poorest and the rest of the population will be greater. Germany and the UK are included for comparison, as examples of EU member countries. These figures change relatively slowly over time.

Table 5.1: Income distribution, % of total income going to poorest 20%, 2000-2012

Brazil	2.9
China	4.7
Germany	8.5
India	8.5
Russia	6.5
UK	5.5

Source: World Bank, World Development Indicators, 2012

It is worth remembering that when China was run on communist lines, health care and education were free. Although the quality of these services was often rather low, they were accessible to all. Nowadays education and health care must be paid for and there are many who have great difficulty finding the necessary cash.

Notice that despite its Communist government, China has a more unequal distribution of income than India. The current Indian government swept to power in 2009 in a reasonably clean democratic election having promised to address the needs of the poor – as had many of its predecessors.

Income distribution has a big impact on the nature of country markets for different types of products. There are quite enough rich people in Shanghai to make it worthwhile for suppliers of luxury products to set up retail outlets, despite the fact that per capita income in China is still relatively low (US$4,940 in 2011). There is also a large middle class that will buy sophisticated products like iPads.

Luxury good sales rise and fall

All through 2012, sales of Europe's exported luxury goods boomed across China. The incomes of the wealthiest were rising fastest of all consumer groups. (In 2005, the figure for the percentage of income going to the poorest was 5.7%.) Fearing a popular backlash, the Chinese government banned TV adverts for expensive watches and the giving of 'gifts' to public officials, in return for favours (a widely used source of corruption). In 2012, luxury sales grew by 20%; in 2013 the growth rate is likely to be in the range 6-8%.

Discussion points

What incentives encourage luxury good businesses to export to China? What risks are they taking in the Chinese market?

Joint ventures

Many foreign markets have individual features that make joint ventures attractive for businesses that have no previous experience there. They are particularly useful wherever language, cultural and political barriers exist. Many foreign businesses that want either to produce or sell in China set up a joint venture with a local partner company. This gives the Chinese government a degree of control over foreign business operations but it can also be helpful to foreign managers who have little experience of China.

Foreign direct investment

FDI has been very important to China. (Data for a range of countries was given in Table 3.1, page 20.) As China became more open to collaboration with foreign partners, FDI became easier to arrange. Joint ventures have often been key features of FDI in China. The link between FDI and the growth of trade shows clearly in Figure 5.2.

FDI has facilitated **technology transfer**. In fact, the Chinese government's wish to acquire new technologies was a driving force in the setting up of many joint ventures. Now, China has a much enhanced research capability and in some fields is capable of conducting its own cutting edge research. It would have been difficult to achieve this without technology transfer in the years following liberalisation.

Figure 5.2: FDI in China

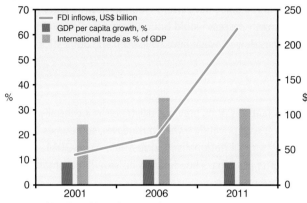

Source: World Bank, World Development Indicators, 2008

Technology transfer refers to the way in which countries with limited access to new technologies may acquire expertise when multinational companies locate there. The foreign company trains local people in the skills that are needed to make use of the new technology. In time, employees are able to move on into other businesses that can use their skills, spreading the new technologies into other sectors.

FDI and technology transfer have been important elements in the spectacular growth of labour productivity (output per person employed) in China. Most people in China are sufficiently well-educated to learn new skills fairly readily. With improved capital equipment and more human capital in place, this increased productivity has contributed substantially to the growth process. Figure 5.3 shows productivity growth for a range of countries. Recent data is hard to find: recession has affected productivity growth.

Figure 5.3: Total factor productivity, average annual growth, 1990-2008, %

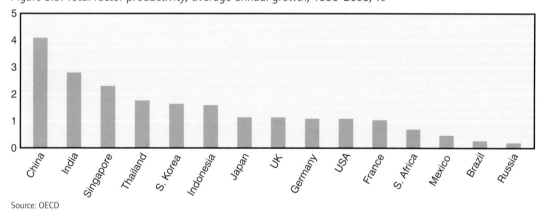

Source: OECD

Trade

China provides a classic example of export-led growth. The development of China has increased competition in world markets and helped suppliers to cut prices for many consumer goods, particularly clothing and toys. This has increased purchasing power for billions of people. Table 5.2 shows how much both exports and imports have grown: China is becoming a very open economy. Invariably, China runs a trade surplus, and reserves of foreign currency have increased dramatically. This has implications for the global economy.

Table 5.2: China's trade balances: exports and imports of goods and services as % of GDP

	2000	2005	2008	2011
Exports	23	37	35	31
Imports	21	32	28	30

Source: World Bank, World Development Indicators, 2013

Many rural Chinese have migrated from the countryside to the cities, where there are job opportunities in the factories creating exports. Their incomes have risen, creating new markets for both domestic output and imports. Any let up in the growth process would bring unemployment and unrest. Recently the flow of migrants from the countryside has slowed, wage rates have risen and domestic consumption is increasing.

State owned enterprises

The Chinese economy still retains features of its previous existence as a centrally planned economy. **State owned enterprises** (SOEs) coexist with privately owned businesses, sometimes in competition with them. SOEs are broadly similar to what we call nationalised industries. As of 2011, SOEs generated 35% of business activity and 43% of profits in China. They tend to be very large organisations: political leaders often try to exert a strong influence on them.

On average, SOEs are less profitable than firms in the private sector: in recent years they have achieved average rates of return on assets of 5%, compared to 8% for the private sector. In sectors where barriers to entry for private firms are low, SOEs face strong competition and make little profit.

> **State owned enterprises** are businesses that are run by the government (local or national). They have often been run in the public interest but are increasingly expected to be profitable.

Chinese government policy now is to reduce the number of SOEs substantially. They remain a very significant part of the Chinese economy. Some are being sold off. Public sector conglomerates are being broken up and encouraged to merge their component parts with private sector producers.

Some SOEs have been very successful. The Aluminium Corporation of China is an SOE that had prospered sufficiently by 2008 to buy a 9% stake in Rio Tinto Zinc, a multinational mining giant which has its head office in the West End of London and interests all over the world. It is not the only SOE that is interested in the prospects for inorganic growth in western markets.

Top executives in SOEs get high pay, sometimes with performance related bonuses. However, some of the most successful companies, like China Mobile, have benefited from their monopoly power. That is changing now that the government has introduced new anti-monopoly laws, which apply to SOEs as much as to the private sector.

A Chinese story

Increasingly, China is able to produce competitively using new technologies. China now has 40% of the world market in photovoltaic (solar) panels – a considerable achievement. But it has not been plain sailing.

Shi Zhengrong went to Australia to study electrical engineering. After his studies were complete he worked for an Australian business that was developing solar panels. In 2001, he was offered US$6 million to go home to Wuxi, just west of Shanghai, and set up his own company. The expectation was that with local government support, cheap land and labour and Mr Shi's expertise, solar panels could be profitable. The company, Suntech, grew.

Suntech achieved a 12% market share in the USA, setting up a production unit in Arizona. This allowed it to sell to customers using public money, (subsidies similar to those offered in the UK), which required them to buy US-made products. Further growth was expected.

Suntech isn't exactly an SOE – but it did have substantial financial backing from the public sector. (Besides the Wuxi council, the China Development Bank and the World Bank contributed.) However, Suntech had many Chinese competitors. Together, they invested so heavily that there is now excess capacity. They still expect further economies of scale and also to develop cheaper technologies that will lead to increased sales in the long run.

Early in 2013, Suntech became insolvent. Besides overcapacity, it had trouble in Arizona. The US government had slapped an import duty on the components that were made in China, then shipped to Arizona for assembly. The Arizona plant will be sold or shut down. As of 2013 the Wuxi city council is trying to rescue the Chinese factories and probably regrets its earlier generosity. Chief Executive Shi has been forced out.

Questions

1. How can a developing country advance so rapidly in terms of its use of new technologies?

2. Why might the owners of these very new companies expect increasing sales in the future?

3. List the mistakes made at Suntech and assess the likely influence that state backing had on company decisions.

Regulation

Regulatory processes are changing in China. Essentially, they are becoming more like those of developed economies. The Chinese government is planning to enforce environmental and employment laws more strictly. The belief is that many small, inefficient enterprises in both the public and the private sector survive by taking little care of their employees and not worrying about pollution controls. Chinese people who have to live near to sources of serious pollution get very upset about the resulting health problems and try hard to protest. The government knows quite well that it has to get the worst polluters to clean up because the health issues are serious.

Competition policy is being tightened up and is being applied to foreign and domestic businesses, including SOEs. This will in time hasten the end of inefficient enterprises. These types of policies will help China to modernise its economy and may well lead to increasing competitiveness in the future. China Mobile, an SOE with 500m subscribers, has faced lawsuits from customers claiming that it abused its monopoly position by charging high prices. The build-up of case law will in time force some businesses to cut prices.

Are there constraints on growth?

Right now, China is catching up with the developed world and this is likely to continue. But some supply constraints are appearing.

- Rising food prices reflect Chinese people's enthusiasm for eating better quality food – more meat and fish.

- Car ownership is rising but it may be difficult to create enough roads fast enough to keep the traffic moving.

- Water is a real problem in the north and west of China, where rainfall is often low. River water is being used for irrigation but there is simply not enough of it to meet the growing demand. Climate change may reduce rainfall further in the dry areas.

- China is having to import more and more of its raw materials to feed its factories and provide energy. The government is busy locating sources all over the world. It is offering some African countries aid money to facilitate the setting up of long term contracts. Commodity prices may rise in response to the increasing demand.

- China has a household registration system called the hukou. It entitles people to welfare benefits and education only in the place where they are registered. Most people who migrate to the city to find work are unable to change their registration – even if their children are born in the city they are still excluded. Migrants run big risks for often low wages and poor quality housing. This is one reason for inequality in China and it could make business expansion and recruitment harder in the future.

Early in 2010 there were reports coming from China of very poor working conditions in many of its factories. It was clear that some employees were working very long hours under difficult conditions, without acceptable safety precautions or adequate breaks, for very low pay.

The Chinese government raised minimum wage levels. Across China there was an attempt to improve working conditions and both pay and consumer spending increased. There have been significant changes. Many people are still working for low pay and in difficult conditions but the improvements are noticeable. China may as a result be a little less competitive than it was. A few businesses in developed countries have gone back to producing close to their own markets – called 'reshoring'.

Discussion point

What do you think might happen to wages in China in the long run? How might this affect businesses and people in the UK?

The impact of recession

China noticed the recession. In 2008 and 2009, the government gave the economy a strong stimulus, by increasing spending and expanding bank lending.

Table 5.3: Comparing recession in China and the developed countries (average)

	GDP growth			Unemployment			Inflation		
	2007	**2008**	**2009**	**2007**	**2008**	**2009**	**2007**	**2008**	**2009***
China	13.0	9.0	8.1	4.0	4.0	n.a.	4.8	5.9	-0.7
Developed countries	2.6	0.5	-3.5	5.7	6.1	8.6	2.1	3.3	0.1

Source: UN, World Economic Situation and Prospects, 2010   *Estimated

The fiscal stimulus worked well. The recession in China was mild by comparison with other economies.

Conclusion

China's growth is dramatic. But the government fears unemployment, just as it fears any threat that seems likely to create political dissent. So long as the Chinese people like the way things are going, the chances are, the majority will be happy with the government and the few that are not can be kept quiet by force. Expect interesting times.

The impact of China on the world economy is sure to be large. But the precise nature of that impact is still far from clear and will depend on the way in which events unfold. Besides, China is not the only fast-growing economy and much depends on what happens elsewhere. The next few chapters will look at other big players and Chapter 20 will look again at China and the world economy.

Chapter 6

Is India catching up?

Iconic companies

Infosys was started up in 1981 in Pune by seven people with US$250 between them for working capital. They were offering IT services to business. In 2012, sales revenue was US$7.4 billion and there were 156,000 employees. The company has branches all over the world and reckons to be able to help make almost any business more efficient. It has world-class capability in the design of IT systems and can find tailor-made solutions to individual problems. Its customers can be anywhere – the systems are designed to fit their precise needs. The programming will often be done in India, because there Infosys can recruit highly trained IT specialists at comparatively low cost. Customers are typically in manufacturing, energy, transport, retailing, finance or healthcare. Of course, a business like this could not develop without the ability to communicate internationally, easily and cheaply.

Infosys now has 32 development centres in India and 55 outside. It has a big programme for improving educational access for Indian children who might otherwise find it difficult to progress to professional jobs. Its strapline is 'powered by intellect, driven by values'.

Tata is a much older company, founded in 1907. It's bigger too – sales revenue was US$100 billion in 2011-12. It has interests worldwide, spread across steel, cars, IT, communications, energy, hotels and tea. (It owns Tetley tea.) Its acquisitions include Corus steel, in 2007, and Jaguar Land Rover in 2008. Tata is based in Mumbai and still run by the Tata family. It is famously philanthropic: one project came up with a software package that can teach illiterate adults to read in 40 hours. Another, following the Asian tsunami of 2004, developed a cheap water purification device.

Questions

1. India has a tradition of corporate social responsibility that is followed by some of its businesses. CSR is rather hard to find in China, although some businesses do make a point of treating employees well, especially if they have scarce skills. How would you account for this contrast?

2. Both Infosys and Tata have a strong record in research and innovation. How would you expect this to help them?

3. Despite their international markets, both companies locate much of their production activity in India. List the pros and cons of this and assess its importance as an element in their success.

India had civilised cities, with piped water and drains, in the bronze age, 4000-5000 years ago. There was much trade and a reliable system of weights and measures. For the times, the economy was very highly developed. Then came successive invasions from the west. The last of these turned India into a British colony. The East India Company became increasingly involved in exploiting economic opportunities and vast profits were made. By 1850, the British-run civil service was in complete control. Although the colonial administration built railways and created an administrative system, economic development at best stagnated and at worst deteriorated during the colonial period. Restrictions on trade made it very difficult for Indian exports to compete with British products.

Quite early on in the twentieth century it became increasingly clear that the people of India would not for long tolerate being a British colony. As the transition process gathered pace, tensions between Hindus and the Muslims deepened. In the end it seemed that partition was inevitable. At independence in 1947, the country split into mainly Hindu India, and mainly Muslim Pakistan. Later in 1972 after a brutal but short war, the eastern part of Pakistan became independent as Bangladesh.

After independence, Indian government policies were based on socialist principles. The objective was to raise standards of living from their dismally low level. For so long India had suffered from a highly unequal distribution of income, with huge numbers of people living at subsistence level, and all too many of those actually starving. Economic policies were designed to ensure that everyone had a reasonable income and to prevent profiteering. Many production decisions were centrally planned by the government. This did not prevent private enterprise in the way that communism did in China, but it did mean the economy was very tightly controlled by bureaucrats. Businesses had to have permission to close down as well as to set up. Sometimes failing businesses were subsidised, using funds that could have been used to help the agricultural sector, which tended to be neglected in favour of secondary production.

The economic logic behind policy making in the decades after independence was based on the concept of self-sufficiency. Indian businesses had long faced difficulties competing with western firms. The idea was to exclude imports, protect domestic producers and build an efficient manufacturing sector behind trade barriers. The economy became much less open, both importing and exporting less, proportionately. The policy didn't work well. Despite some rather slow growth, by the 1980s, the vast majority of Indians remained dismally poor.

Making changes

The cost of import substitution policies gradually became clear. While the Indian economy was growing at an average 2% per year, the Asian tigers, South Korea and Taiwan, Thailand and Indonesia were growing much faster. This happened despite the fact that the Green Revolution in agriculture had had considerable impact in India. (This involved using new types of seed and better irrigation to increase crop sizes.) The Indian government could see that bureaucratic control had stifled enterprise.

During the 1990s many government controls on businesses were removed. Some Indian businesses began to succeed internationally. Recently some have grown dramatically fast and been spectacularly innovative – like Tata and Infosys in the case study above. Education in India was of variable quality for a long time but it did exist and some of it was very good compared to that of other countries with similar per capita incomes. In time India's human capital became a valuable resource. India now has an **open economy** and its growing export markets lead to job creation. Exports as a percentage of GDP rose from 13% in 2000 to 24% in 2012. Figure 6.1 shows Indian export growth compared to world export growth.

> **Open economy:** one in which exports and imports form a significant proportion of GDP. In addition there will be capital movements both in and out of the country and technology transfer.

Figure 6.1: Export growth, 1991–2011

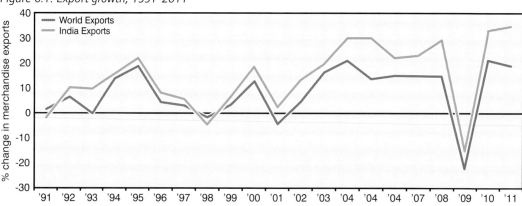

Source: IMF

By 2013, India's IT sector had annual sales revenue of US$100 billion, mostly from customers abroad. Not for nothing is it called 'the west's back office'. IBM, Dell and JPMorgan all employ thousands of professionals in India. Altogether there are 1.6 million people working in IT, most of them graduates and mostly

English speaking. India has a reputation for providing high quality services in this field. Even so there are still many unemployed graduates in India. It is expected that in the near future, there will be scope for rapid growth in research generally and in pharmaceuticals, electronics, cars and aerospace. Biotechnology is another promising area. All these sectors want to recruit well-educated employees.

Key features of the economy

India's population stands at 1.2 billion and is still growing by 1.4% per year. In most countries, population growth slows when incomes rise and women have opportunities to work. Poverty is still far too widespread in India for population growth to drop the way it has in China, Thailand and Indonesia. Table 6.1 shows changes in India's GDP per capita at **purchasing power parity**, compared to that of China.

> **Purchasing power parity** refers to an exchange rate that has been adjusted to allow accurate comparisons of purchasing power. It is used because prices for specific products vary considerably between countries and consequently so does the purchasing power of a given sum of money.

Table 6.1: GDP per capita, US$

	Per capita GDP, PPP, 2011	Average annual growth of real per capita income, 2000-2011
India	US$3,620	7.8%
China	US$8,390	10.8%

Source: World Bank, World Development Indicators 2013

Take a look at Figure 5.1 (page 29), which shows economic growth for the BRIC countries. There is much talk of India catching up with China and India has clearly been helped by the relatively small slowdown in the growth rate during the recession, 2008-09. You might argue that Indians on average have a better quality of life than the Chinese because there are far fewer restrictions on personal freedom in India than there are in China and because India has a more equal distribution of income. But the economic difference is still striking.

Productivity, savings and investment

With abundant labour and relatively little capital equipment, productivity, i.e. output per person employed, is still very low in India. In part this reflects the fact that large numbers of people are still living on the land, farming with little cash for investment in farm machinery or improved irrigation. However, although productivity is starting from a low base, it is now rising very fast. The government is trying hard to support farmers' efforts to increase the size of their crops. In manufacturing and parts of the service sector, investment is strong and increased productivity is contributing to economic growth. (See Figure 5.3 page 31.) Figure 6.2 shows savings and investment growth. The sharp rise in savings and investment from 2002 onwards levelled off after 2008, but at around 35%, it remained high.

Figure 6.2: Savings and Investment, % of GDP, 1992-2008

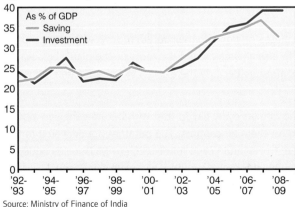

Source: Ministry of Finance of India

Annual FDI in India is much less than in the other BRIC countries (see Table 3.1, page 20), reflecting the old political objective of making India self-sufficient. Efforts are now being made to increase the flow of FDI by building foreign confidence in the economy. Also there are internal funds available for investment because India's savings rate is very high. Productivity can be expected to continue increasing as production becomes more capital intensive.

Signs of progress

- Increasing use of mobile phones is known to be having a positive effect on the growth rate. They raise farm incomes by giving farmers better information on where and when to take their products to market. Finding the best market has potential to reduce the amount of food that goes to waste as well.

- Whereas it used to take 71 days to start a new business in 2005, by 2012 this had been reduced to 27 days.

- Investment is high, indicating rapid growth potential.

- The fiscal stimulus designed by the government to counteract the effects of recession seems to have worked fairly well – growth sank no lower than 4%. However, as of 2013, the chances of high growth rates look uncertain. As always, growth depends partly on the annual monsoon rains providing for good crops.

McDonalds and McCains: a supply chain story

McDonalds is everywhere, even in India. All those IT workers need fast food. You might not expect beefburgers to go down well in India, where the Hindu majority will not kill cattle. So beanburgers and McNuggets must be important. With fries.

When McDonalds explored the possibilities of opening in India, they looked at the locally grown potatoes and found they were unsuitable for making fries. So they began talking with McCains. They have experience of finding ways to grow potatoes for chip-making in many different countries.

But even they thought that it couldn't be done in India. They would have to persuade the farmers to grow the right varieties, get them to irrigate the crops economically, train them to approach the whole process differently from the way their past experience suggested. How could they possibly do this? The Indian government used to run advisory services for farmers but investment in agriculture had been shrinking for years, because the government faced a rising bill for its subsidies for food, fuel and fertiliser. So no help was available from that source.

McCains started out with research projects. It persuaded a few farmers in Gujarat province to work with it by planting new varieties of potatoes, and provided guidance on growing and harvesting them. Farmers typically sell their produce to government agencies that are carefully regulated in order to protect farmers from rogue traders. McCains paid the farmers a guaranteed price for the crop that was higher than they could get in the regulated market. In this way, McCains discovered what varieties grew best and how to get a good crop. Then they recruited farmers to their project in greater numbers.

They insisted that farmers must stop flooding their potato furrows with water and use drip irrigation. This feeds water straight to a small area around the roots of the plant. Less water is required but the plants get more of the moisture because there is less evaporation and reduced humidity means fewer pests.

McCains experts visited the farmers every day to start with but now they go much less often. They have 400 farmers working for them on contract. The potatoes are delivered to the McCains plant where they are sliced, fried, frozen and boxed for dispatch to McDonalds outlets. The farmers are laughing. Some of them are buying cars, even those with very small farms.

So what's wrong?

You could argue, nothing. In 2012, its worst year since 2007, India's growth rate sank only to +4%. The prospects for the future are very promising. But you might also argue that 25% of Indians are still living below the poverty line, i.e. US$1.25 a day at purchasing power parity. Many more do better than that but are still poor by any standards, despite substantial progress in recent years. What are the problems?

- Some bureaucratic controls remain. In particular, regulated markets sometimes prevent the price signalling mechanism from working to show where scarce resources can be used most efficiently. Controlled prices designed to provide cheap food for the urban poor give farmers little incentive to invest in increasing output.

- Government subsidies, designed to make fuel and fertiliser available to poor farmers, have been very costly. The money might be more effectively spent in other ways.

- Shopkeepers who sell subsidised products to poor people sometimes adulterate the product so that they can sell some of it on the open market where prices are higher. This is not helping poor people.

- The financial sector is still poorly developed. Few people have bank accounts and many cannot get access to the credit they need to fund investment.

Doing something to help the large number of poor farmers remains a high priority for the government. Researchers are looking at traditional policies and asking questions. New ideas are needed. The government's chief economic adviser has said that the poorest 20% of the population should get at least 20% of any increase in GDP. This is much more than is typical in any country. Usually, although growing GDP does benefit poor people, it will help them less than it helps the rich. So arranging for them to benefit proportionately is innovative.

Since 2010, the Indian government has raised spending on health, education and welfare provision for the poor. Food subsidies are being increased. This will be expensive but politically popular, although care must be taken because past efforts to provide subsidised food have sometimes led to widespread corruption. However, together with farmers using mobile phones to find the best market prices, these measures could really help to reduce inequality further.

Irrigation is carefully controlled too. But this gives the power to distribute the water to local officials. The farmers who get it have no incentive to use it sparingly. If water were priced somewhere near its market value, increased use of drip-feed systems might mean that the scarce water supplies could be used more efficiently. This would increase rural productivity.

Other policies include steady progress on privatisation and improved banking services. Once farm incomes improve, spending power will rise, creating a growing market for the output of the secondary sector and possibilities for global exports. Optimism could bring along a self-fulfilling prophecy. Rising incomes would mean rising tax revenues and more money to spend on infrastructure. That would ease some more bottlenecks – Bangalore is famously congested.

Prosperity is not evenly spread across the whole country. The poorest seven states have 40% of the population. In these states, standards of living are similar to those in many African countries. Measures to help the agricultural sector may help these states to develop.

Chapter 7

Which other countries are making waves?

Brazil's exports

Vale started life in 1943 when the Brazilian government set it up as a public sector mining operation. It was privatised in 1997. It is now a multinational and the second largest mining company in the world. It produces 85% of Brazil's output of iron ore and has diversified into steel, energy, fertilisers and road and rail transport. It has been the world's biggest producer and exporter of iron ore for some time. Though Vale bought many other companies, there has also been much organic growth, involving the rapid development of new investment projects. Developing countries' need for extensive investment in infrastructure projects has created a huge market for Vale's mineral products. The company has a tradition of moving swiftly to develop new markets before the competition arrives.

Besides mineral products, Brazil also exports agricultural products. It is the world's largest exporter of coffee, sugar, chickens, beef and orange juice. Offshore oil reserves are now being developed. There is plenty of it, but it is 7000m down, beneath the sea and layers of hard rock. The cost of extraction will be high but if oil prices stay high, it will be very profitable.

Some of Brazil's success rests on the economic policies adopted since the mid-1990s, which have made it into a social democratic market economy. Conventional macroeconomic policies have kept the economy fairly stable and helped to create many new jobs. It is estimated that 20 million Brazilians emerged from poverty in just six years, out of a total population of 200 million, between 2002 and 2008. Half the population is now described as having middle incomes. Besides the new jobs, new welfare policies are at last helping to tackle Brazil's very unequal income distribution. (See Table 5.1 page 30.)

Questions

1. How have recent developments in the global economy helped Brazilian businesses to export?

2. What effect will rising incomes have on business profits?

3. How does stability help economic growth?

4. To what extent might changing commodity prices affect Brazil?

Brazil, Russia, India and China, the BRIC countries, have collectively distinguished themselves in recent years because they are soon to provide more than half of global GDP growth. Figure 7.1 shows their contribution compared with that of the G7 – the US, UK, Japan, Germany France, Italy and Canada.

Figure 7.1: Contributions to GDP growth: the BRICs v the G7

Share of global GDP growth
(%, based on purchasing power parity $ terms)

Bric countries

1990-2000	2000-2008	2008-2014*
32.2%	46.3%	61.3%

G7 countries – US, UK, Japan, Germany, Canada, France and Italy

41.1%	19.8%	12.8%

GDP per capita
(purchasing power parity $)

Bric countries

2000	2014*
$2,618	← $8,654

G7 countries

2000	2014*
$29,651	← $45,780

Source: IMF   *Estimates

The term 'BRIC countries' came from an employee of Goldman Sachs, the bankers – but it has stuck. The BRICs are all emerging markets that are geographically large, have big populations and quite diversified economies. But in all other ways, they are each very different from one another. China is notable for its openness to trade. India is less developed than China, except in IT and business services, but may to a degree catch up over the next few years. Brazil has some successful manufacturers but is above all a commodity exporting economy, benefiting from the competitiveness of its mining and agricultural sectors. (Vale is part of this.) Russia has potential in manufacturing but actually relies heavily on sales of oil and gas. In each case, growth has resulted from very different circumstances. The data in Table 7.1 shows some differences. Indonesia and S. Korea are included for comparison; S. Korea experienced rapid growth during the 1980s and is now regarded as being so successful that it is a developed country – notice the modest rate of economic growth as the economy approaches maturity. Indonesia has had high growth rates for some years; in terms of population it is the third largest Asian country. Notice also the big variations between these economies as to the amounts of GDP accounted for by investment and exports.

Table 7.1: Some international comparisons, 2011

	Brazil	Russia	India	China	S. Africa	Indonesia	S. Korea
GDP, US$, bn	2,108	1,522	1,766	6,643	352	713	1,039
GDP per capita, US$, PPP	11,420	21,210	3,620	8,390	10,710	4,500	29,920
Population, mn	197	143	1,241	1,344	51	242	50
Economic growth, %	2.7	4.3	6.3	9.3	3.1	6.5	3.6
Mobile phones per 100 people	137	155	70	85	118	109	108
Income share, lowest 20%	2.9	6.5	8.5	4.7	2.7	7.6	n/a
HDI ranking	85	55	136	101	121	121	12
Investment growth, %	5.5	7.5	13.1	13.5	7.6	6.4	2.0
Exports, % of GDP	14	38	19	31	31	31	62

Source: World Bank, World Development Indicators, 2012

Questions

1. To what extent have the BRIC countries affected competition in global markets?

2. What opportunities has growth in the BRICs created for G7 businesses?

3. Assess the effect of these trends on incomes in the BRIC countries.

Growing so fast, the BRICs have increasing economic power and influence in the global economy. The long term impact of this is very uncertain. China has a trade surplus and is an active source of FDI for the rest of the world. The USA has a big trade deficit, and China has lent vast sums to the US government which have offset the deficit. Changing this potentially unstable situation will be difficult and take time.

Brazil

Natural resources are not essential for economic growth. Japan developed a high standard of living while importing most of the natural resources it needed. But Brazil illustrates the value that natural resources can have – as shown in the opening case study. Partly it is simply that Brazil is geographically big – almost the size of China, but with a much smaller population.

There is potential vulnerability for any economy that relies on commodity exports in that their raw material prices can be very volatile. In recent years rising commodity prices have been of great benefit. That may continue, but in the past, falling commodity prices have been a problem for many countries that depended on them.

None of this is visible in Table 7.1. Yet the growth of the Brazilian middle class is impressive and even the poorest have experienced some benefits: government policy has provided for cash transfers to the 12 million poorest people. Although Brazil still has one of the world's most unequal income distributions, it is becoming less so. Growth in the provision of pensions and public sector services has helped too.

The emerging middle class make good customers. Consumer credit is growing and many businesses are attracted by the growing markets. However there are no big car manufacturers producing for export and Brazil has no particular lead in high-tech products. Brazil spends little on R&D. S. Korea, with a population that is one quarter of the size of Brazil's, habitually registers 30 times as many patents. Brazil is a land of contrasts, a successful democracy with no wars and sophisticated economic policies. But there is still much corruption and the government seems unable to stop the destruction of the rain forests. 17% of homes still have no running water. And if you want to start up a new business it will take a whopping 119 days to complete the administrative process. No other country on our list comes anywhere near that. (In the UK, it takes 13 days). Yet if everything goes well, standards of living in Brazil could improve very quickly.

In Asian countries that have experienced rapid economic growth, the high rates of savings and investment are often cited as causes of growth. Brazilians are not keen savers and that means fewer funds for investment. Brazil's 19% of GDP spent on investment is similar to levels of investment in the UK and the USA. As you might expect, the growth rate is lower than growth rates in India and China. You could argue that the figures for 2011 are still distorted by recession. Brazil remains the sixth largest economy in the world with possibilities for rapid growth in the future.

Russia

The Russian economy still bears some of the scars of seventy years of Communism, followed by a breakneck transition to a market economy. From 1917 until 1989, the economy of the then USSR was **centrally planned**, with next to no activity in the private sector. To start with, the planners were quite successful in mobilising resources for investment and Russia was generally classified as a developed country. It was the USSR that started the 'space race', giving its many scientists the opportunity to put the first satellite into orbit in 1957, and soon after, the first manned space mission. (This worried the Americans mightily and led in the end to the moon landings.)

> **Centrally planned economies** were those in which all or most economic decisions were taken by governments. Planning involved deciding on the inputs to be used, the production targets and the prices of all products.

In the decades following World War II, the gap between standards of living in the Communist countries and those in the West became more and more obvious. Russians were told that most people in the West were living on very low pay, while being exploited by a small number of seriously rich capitalists. In time though the government of the USSR wanted to send their many scientists and other scholars to conferences in the west, where they could learn about the technological changes that were taking place. These people went home with stories of ordinary people with pleasant homes and cars and holiday plans. They realised that the stories of very low standards of living in the West were lies.

When the iron curtain came down in 1989, each country had to decide what to do with its nationalised industries. In Russia, vouchers were given to every member of the population, and these could be exchanged for shares in the nation's industries. However, for several years after 1989 these industries were struggling. They were producing low quality goods that could not compete on world markets. Sales revenue was falling and many of the workers were not getting paid regularly. Many people sold their vouchers for whatever they could get for them, often just to buy desperately needed food.

People with money could buy the vouchers and use them to take over whole organisations, factories, farms, mines and oil wells, for relatively small sums of money. As these individuals accumulated productive assets, they soon had funds coming in and could buy more vouchers and more shares. They became known as oligarchs, a small group of people who had close links to the government and were of sometimes doubtful honesty. Eventually some of them fell out with the government. A few ended up behind bars in Russia. Some got their money out of Russia and ended up living abroad, buying football clubs and palatial homes. Many others stayed in Russia and got on with the job of running their businesses. Not surprisingly, corruption remains a serious problem.

GDP fell substantially after 1989 but after about 7 years, things began to improve. Jobs were created, wages were paid on time and the newly privatised industries became much more efficient and began to make profits. Ordinary people began to notice a difference. Some of them opened their own small businesses and did well if they could meet consumers' needs. Despite many problems, steady growth became the norm. However, many of the old industries had to close down. They could not adapt to competing on world markets and their old-fashioned capital equipment kept production costs high. Russia still has difficulty producing competitive consumer goods but imports can be paid for with the proceeds from exports of oil and gas.

So long as energy prices stay relatively high, Russia will prosper. However, it may be that many oil-producing countries will expand oil supplies substantially in the next few years. And in the US, large new finds of shale gas are reducing dependence on imports. Energy prices may stay high, as demand increases in developing countries, or they may fall as new finds meet the rising demand. This of course could slow Russia's economic growth considerably. However, Russia has a long tradition of excellence in both science and the arts and many Russians are well educated. If their potential for research and product design are harnessed effectively, it should be possible to diversify the economy. Before the Revolution in 1917, the economy was developing in similar ways to Germany, the USA and the UK. Under favourable circumstances it might well catch up again.

As of 2013, President Putin was expecting economic growth of 5-6%. This could be achieved, given Russia's advantages and a favourable world economy. It has been suggested that it will not be, because Russia is currently the 120th best place in the world to do business, according to the World Bank's 2012 rankings. Mr Putin wants Russia to be 20th by 2018. This would involve major changes in the business environment, especially in the protection of property rights and the rule of law. If the Russian economy is to grow, it needs a strong legal framework.

Russia still has problems with corruption. Also, the difficulty of establishing legal rights makes the country look like a risky place to invest. Strong economic growth requires investment in small and medium sized businesses but the risks discourage potential entrepreneurs. Foreign direct investment would help too but in 2011-12 more capital was flowing out of Russia than in. It appears that for now, neither foreigners nor Russians see it as a particularly good place to invest.

New businesses

In 1998, Galina Popova set up her own travel agency in Moscow. She had noticed that many people wanted to take holidays in western Europe and north Africa, but knew nothing about how to arrange it. Her husband had worked in the UK for six months and she had used the time to get fluent in English. She organised package tours that were just right for Russians who hadn't learnt much English and didn't want to make complicated bookings with airlines and hotels. To start with she was the tour guide as well as the organiser but she was soon able to expand and took on four employees.

Questions

1. What was happening in Russia at the time that made it possible for Galina to succeed?

2. Ten years later, Galina and her husband and two grown-up sons were still living in a two bedroom flat in a pleasant but not luxurious flat in a Moscow suburb. Why might this be?

South Africa is the most prosperous economy in Africa and has enormous potential.

Which other countries are prospering?

The South African government thinks it should be included in the BRICS. It is the most prosperous economy in Africa and has enormous potential. It is resource rich and has much more human capital than most African countries. But it carries a heavy burden in the shape of the 18% of young adults who are HIV positive. Unemployment is high and the government has to work out how to help the large numbers of people who have not in the past benefited from economic development. The distribution of income is fairer than it used to be but many black South Africans remain dismally poor.

The four Asian Tigers grew very fast in the 1980s and 1990s. Taiwan, South Korea and Singapore are now generally seen as developed countries, no longer a part of the 'Third World'. Hong Kong is once more part of China, though with its own legal structure that preserves some of the features of its time as a British colony. This group was part of a much larger group, the newly industrialised economies, or NIEs. This includes Mexico, Thailand, Indonesia, Malaysia and other highly successful countries that have enlarged their manufacturing sectors, greatly improving standards of living.

Each of these countries has a different history, and often traces of the historic situation remain visible in their economies. There is no single recipe for growth that is applicable to all. Each one has allocated resources in a different way. Success seems to depend on identifying the problems and the opportunities accurately.

All are now outward-looking economies that have become steadily more open to imports, while exporting vigorously. But some are much more open than others: the Asian economies in particular. Some countries – e.g. South Africa – seem to be getting great benefits from increasing use of mobile phones. Their impact in Africa generally is exciting – but China managed to take off without them. It looks as though all countries that still have large agricultural sectors can benefit from investment in ways of increasing agricultural productivity. But essentially, there are many different routes to prosperity, and they vary, depending on the strengths and weaknesses of the individual economy.

Chapter 8

Is there a market?

LVMH

"There are four main elements in our business model – product, distribution, communication and price," said one executive at Louis Vuitton:Möet Hennessy, the luxury brands group. He went on: "Our job is to do such a fantastic job on the first three that people forget all about the fourth." The business strategy focuses on designing the perfect shop and advertising in artful ways and the customers really do seem to forget about the prices. LVMH never reduces prices during a sale. Instead it moves stock to where it is likely to sell best or, as a last resort, it destroys stocks that won't sell. It does not allow manufacturing of its designs under licence either – everything is produced in-house.

Until about 2005, Vuitton, the leather goods core of the company, depended heavily on the Japanese market. That had been one place where customers really did seem not to look at the price tag. Since then, demand has fallen away as younger Japanese women sought out more individual brands. The company turned increasingly to China. In 2009, 18% of Vuitton's revenue came from China. Bernard Arnault, the chair and CEO of LVMH said "We treat the Chinese customer as being very sophisticated." The key element in the LVMH marketing strategy was to treat China just like any other market. So choosing the best location for the shops and giving them expensive fittings is all part of the image construction. Vuitton is now expanding successfully in Mongolia.

Vuitton executives always take the mayor out to lunch if they think there may be a possibility that they might want to expand in another Chinese city.

LVMH survived the 2008-10 recession remarkably well and part of this success had to do with the steadiness of the Chinese market.

Questions

1. Why does this strategy work for LVMH?

2. What other countries might have markets that would be of interest to LVMH?

3. Would this strategy work for other types of businesses?

4. How might EADS, the manufacturer of Airbuses, approach the Chinese market? What differences would there be between their approach and that of LVMH?

5. The Chinese government recently tried to ban the giving of gifts in return for favours from government officials. How might this affect LVMH?

Deciding whether to set up shop in a new market is complicated. Businesses may be aware that they are reaching saturation in their existing markets. They may be actively looking for new export markets. And yet, how can they be sure that venturing into new territory will be a success?

Part of the answer lies in following tried and tested marketing strategies. However, these will have to be planned to suit the situation – a hitherto unknown market. This chapter looks at the ways in which conventional marketing approaches could be made to work in an unfamiliar setting. Chapter 9 goes on to cover issues relating to the business environment in the market concerned, the costs and the practicalities of getting started and the ways in which the inevitable risks might be minimised. It takes a longer view, one in which the business will not just sell its product but also become a long term presence in the economy and perhaps invest in production there.

The case study on Louis Vuitton is all about an approach that is comparatively simple. The business with a strong brand and a big reputation, producing a status symbol that says to onlookers, 'I'm rich', will succeed if incomes are growing fast. Many countries that have recent or current experience of serious poverty have growing middle classes, groups of people who are enjoying their new-found prosperity. The chance to buy branded consumer goods is highly attractive. However, many sellers of such goods may already have moved into the market. Market shares may already be an issue. How can the newcomer be sure to capture a significant slice of the market?

Market analysis

Wherever anyone is doing business, there is just no substitute for acquiring a good knowledge of the market. We know how this is done in our own markets – marketing specialists will do their research. They will undertake surveys, set up focus groups, look for secondary data that may help and write reports. But how would you start this process in a foreign country? Often the key element in the process is identifying potential employees who could actually help. Fedders, the air conditioning people (see page 12), hired a few Chinese people who were living and working in the USA, but were able and willing to look for possible joint venture partners in China. Many UK businesses start out by looking for export markets in English-speaking countries.

Secondary data will provide information on income growth and income distribution. The latter is especially important for businesses hoping to sell consumer goods. Quite poor countries may have some very wealthy people who may buy luxury goods in quantities that could justify the setting up of retail outlets. On the other hand, a more equal distribution of income will mean fewer consumers with big spending power. Some exporters will want to know if there is a significant middle class developing. Similarly, the degree of urbanisation may be important – so data on the percentage of people living in urban areas may be useful. Quantitative data of this kind will provide clues as to which items in the product range might be of interest in the market concerned.

Where are the gaps?

In some markets, other exporters may already be active. Is there room for another similar business? How competitive is the market likely to be? During the 1990s, western businesses piled into China at an astonishing rate. They all felt they needed to get a piece of the action in the world's most populous country. They didn't seem to realise that most of China's people had very little money to spend, and that setting up a business in China involves negotiating with local government and Communist party officials. Some of them made significant losses. Some stayed on anyway, for the long term benefits.

Identifying a gap in the market reduces the likelihood of losses in an unfamiliar situation. This means investigating market segments and looking at existing sellers in each one. Finding a gap can lead to the identification of a target market.

Targeting the market

Qualitative market research can indicate what potential customers might actually want to buy. **Consumer profiles** may be needed. Here cultural awareness becomes critical. This is where joint ventures and local contacts can be invaluable.

> **Consumer profiles** define the characteristics of customers within a market segment. These may be based on age, income, tastes and interests, hobbies, shopping habits or any other feature of the market segment.

For Louis Vuitton, the key market segment was Chinese people working in the private sector and earning high salaries. In fact, they knew a lot about their potential customers because their US, Asian and European outlets were already selling to Chinese people who could afford to travel. They were able to identify the items in their diversified range that could best be marketed inside mainland China.

Some suppliers of luxury products charge more for them in the Chinese market than elsewhere, because their customers appear not to be very sensitive to price levels. This could reflect the fact that higher prices carry a bigger message about the status of the buyer. But this just emphasises the need for businesses to be thoroughly familiar with customer profiles in the market segment they are targeting. Setting the price too high could be disastrous for profits. They need to know something about the elasticity of demand in the target market.

Market mapping

Some products may need to be adapted for a particular market, taking due account of local preferences and habits. Identifying a gap in the market means looking at the existing market and how it is catered for by the businesses that are already selling.

VW in China

VW has been highly successful in China. Early on in the liberalisation process, in the late 1980s, it negotiated two joint ventures and became a major supplier to the Chinese government. At one point in the 1990s it had 70% of the Chinese market. It targeted the market for fleet cars and taxis and for many years all Shanghai's taxis were VWs. Then the big Asian carmakers arrived. Technology transfer meant that Chinese car producers began to compete too. By 2009, VW supplied just 1.4 million of the 6.3 million vehicles sold in China.

In the late 1990s, the emerging group of very wealthy Chinese sought to buy luxury cars, such as BMW, Mercedes, Audi, Ferrari and Porsche. Then VW and their competitors expected a big middle class to emerge, creating a fast growing market. To start with, this growth was actually quite slow. Luxury cars were heavily taxed and the newly prosperous people on middle incomes were looking for cars priced as competitively as possible. Aggressive price cutting and rising incomes meant that after 2004, this market began to grow spectacularly. But some carmakers found profits falling as they tried to compete. The Chinese carmaker, Chery, could produce its QQ micro-car for around $4,000 and in 2006, its sales went up by 136%.

By 2007, VW could see its position declining. It decided to launch ten new models designed specifically for the Chinese market. In particular, it planned an electric version of its Golf-based Lavida model. It also planned to work hard to increase brand recognition and to meet specific Chinese needs. (For example, prestigious customers in China will normally have a driver and sit in the back, so back seats need to be spacious and comfortable.)

Competition in the market for cheap cars in China is keeping prices low. But VW's premium models are doing really well. In total, VW is selling 2 million cars a year there. China is the world's biggest car market; as of 2012, VW had 18% of it and profits are rising. Their target for 2018 is sales of 4 million a year.

Unlike Toyota, VW gives little attention to the production process. Instead, it keeps costs down by using the minimum number of common 'platforms', i.e. using the same basic framework for as many models as possible. Another way VW keeps costs down is to use the same parts on many different models. The company has a culture of permanent innovation, willingness to take risks and very careful attention to detail.

VW could be vulnerable to a downturn in Chinese spending. But with its huge range of models designed specifically for the Chinese market, it may continue to thrive there.

Questions

1. What are the key reasons for VW's success in China?

2. VW faces strong competition. What strategies might protect it in a downturn?

A Jac plug-in hybrid car on display at a Beijing motor show in 2010. The Chinese government wants to encourage use of these cars to reduce pollution.

Market mapping uses a two dimensional diagram to show how the market perceives a range of competing products. Two key characteristics can be used for each market map – these could be price and some aspect of quality. The relevant features will vary according to the product. The competing producers can then be identified on the grid, showing how each relates to key features of the market. Figure 8.1 shows a market mapping for car brands in China. By 2006, the VW Santana, its Chinese cash cow, as common a taxi in Shanghai as a black cab in London, was looking outdated and poor value. The Japanese carmakers were doing better with their usual combination of quality and reliability at a moderate price, while the local Chinese businesses were competing well in the very price sensitive segment of the market.

VW needed to reposition itself. Designing specific models to suit the Chinese market helped, and targeting the market for electric cars opened up newer market segments. Designing new premium models that closely fitted Chinese needs and could compete with Toyota, BMW and others was a strategy that worked well.

Figure 8.1: Market mapping for cars in China, 2006

> **Market mapping** places competing producers or products on a grid that shows how the market perceives each in relation to two market characteristics. The vertical comparison might relate to price or age groups. The horizontal comparison might relate to perceptions based on image, e.g. functional as opposed to aspirational, fashionable or luxury images that the product might have.

Market positioning

Market mapping involves identifying the various segments in the market and the key differences between their respective requirements. Businesses then look for those market segments where there could be opportunities for new or differentiated products. Where there are many competing producers already offering a wide choice to consumers, competition will mean that profit margins tend to be modest. **Market positioning** involves devising a product that will attract a particular market segment that is currently not so well catered for. Having a range of products, or models (in VW's case), strategically positioned to cover as much of the potential market as possible, will maximise sales.

> **Market positioning** defines products according to likely customer perceptions of their selling points. It allows the business to analyse the market in terms of the key characteristics that define different market segments.

Obviously, doing the market research that enables the business to assess the attractiveness of a foreign market in this way involves heavy investment. It requires careful observation over a period of time and risks will have to be taken. That does not mean that small businesses are excluded from exporting to emerging markets. They can use local partners to take care of the distribution functions and find appropriate markets. That said, market orientation, which leads businesses to study the needs of the target market with great care, requires both resources and long term commitment.

Is it worth it?

Once businesses have a clear vision of their potential markets, they can begin to estimate possible future sales revenue and likely costs. With an estimated future income stream they can use investment appraisal techniques to evaluate the likely profitability of their planned ventures. Estimates of profit can be set against the initial investment to determine which products have the best rates of return and the most promising outlook. However, in new markets the risks and uncertainties may be very significant.

Large businesses are very much attracted to fast growing markets. But these are likely also to be unpredictable markets. Careful market research simply helps to reduce this uncertainty but it can never eliminate it.

This chapter has looked at market attractiveness in the context of China. However, similar principles can be followed in many countries that have experienced rapid economic growth. Identifying and examining all the relevant factors that could affect the market is important in helping businesses to avoid losses when reaching out to unfamiliar markets.

Chapter 9

Which locations are most attractive?

JCB

Iconic status belongs to those businesses that give their owner's name to the product. JCB are up there with Hoover and Kleenex, possibly proving themselves to be even more durable. In 2009, they made a loss and cut their global workforce from 9,500 to 7,000. Construction is always among the very hardest hit in a recession, and during 2008 their order book was at one point down by 75% from the previous year. Nevertheless, in 2009 JCB, still a family-owned business, got their 25th Queen's Award for Enterprise.

In 2012, JCB made their highest ever profit. In early 2013 they took on 500 more employees at their headquarters in Staffordshire. Chairman Sir Anthony Bamford said:

> "In view of the continued fragility of the global economy, which has led to renewed slow-downs in emerging and developed markets, JCB's results in 2012 are extremely encouraging. They not only demonstrate the resilience of our business, but highlight the importance of continued investment in products, facilities and customer service."

JCB sells in 150 countries and has 1,500 dealer depots across the world. They offer customer support which is a vital part of the package. It's the fifth largest manufacturer of construction equipment in the world and has 18 factories altogether, including those in India, China, the USA, Brazil and Germany. Production is based on 'meticulous design, rigorous testing and best practice lean manufacturing techniques'.

The company has been no slouch when it comes to outsourcing. Two thirds of component inputs are bought outside the UK, for example from Spain, Sweden, Germany, China, India and Slovakia. The company would like to import fewer components but buys where the engineering skills are the best.

JCB has been in India since 1979. At that time, it didn't look like a brilliant market. The abundant cheap labour meant that people were shifting rocks and soil, most of the time. Women carried it on their heads. They still do – they need the work. But the pace at which India is developing, and its pressing need for improved infrastructure, is creating a strong market for construction equipment. Since 2004 demand has been growing dramatically and India's shallow recession helps to explain why the company survived 2009 in reasonable health.

There are two JCB factories in India with a third opening in Jaipur in 2014. New roads are urgently needed and machines are needed to build them quickly. JCB assembles some of its products in India and trains drivers to operate them, as well as the maintenance crews. The government is making infrastructure building a high priority and the outlook for JCB is very promising.

Setting up production and distribution facilities in India posed relatively few problems for JCB. They have a loyal workforce there and a long track record. They were prepared to operate on a small scale for as long as it took. When India's economic growth rate started to soar, they were well-placed to meet the demand. JCB is still family owned.

Questions

1. What are the key elements in JCB's success to date?

2. What information would JCB have needed to help to make the decision about whether or not to invest in their own factories in India?

3. JCB face strong competition in Asia from Japanese producers such as Hitachi and Komatsu. Assess two ways in which they might try to minimise the threat.

The business environment

When the intention is to go beyond just selling some exports, to develop a strong presence in a foreign market and to locate some of the production process there, very careful investigation is needed to establish how workable the proposal is. This must include making some comparisons between a range of suitable locations.

When China was opening up to the outside world in the 1980s and 1990s, many businesses simply saw the world's biggest market, with its 1.3 billion potential consumers. None of them wanted to be left behind. But then the difficulties became apparent. At least 500 million Chinese are still depressingly poor. They have enough to eat and they have clothing and shelter, all the basics, but they are not exactly a marketing manager's dream. Now many businesses are eyeing India in the same way, but there is an even bigger problem – its per capita income is still well below China's.

Size, economic growth and wealth are not the only important criteria. There are many important questions that must be investigated if a proper investment appraisal is undertaken.

How well-developed is the country?

Development goes hand in hand with income growth. But there are measures of development that can be helpful in providing a wider view. The **Human Development Index** can be useful because it ranks countries in relation to several aspects of development. It has three strands including income as measured by GDP per capita and life expectancy. The third strand measures access to education, using adult literacy rates and percentages of age groups enrolled in schools. The HDI provides an indication of the extent to which rising incomes are having an impact throughout the population. Access to education is a particularly important indicator for businesses that will want to hire skilled labour.

> The **Human Development Index** is constructed by the United Nations Development Program and provides a measure of development based on access to health care and education as well as national income. It therefore includes qualitative as well as quantitative aspects of development.

Table 9.1 shows HDI rankings and figures for selected countries. The BRICs all score quite well. Those in the low income category have serious problems that would probably deter most businesses. Only the oil and the mining companies would be likely to proceed in spite of those problems. Although recently, mobile phone operators have done well in the most adverse scenarios.

Table 9.1: The HDI in selected countries, 2012

World ranking	Country	Index	World ranking	Country	Index
VERY HIGH DEVELOPMENT			**HIGH DEVELOPMENT**		
1	Norway	.955	55	Russia	.788
3	USA	.937	61	Mexico	.775
12	Korea	.909	64	Malaysia	.769
20	France	.893	85	Brazil	.730
26	UK	.875	90	Turkey	.722
MEDIUM DEVELOPMENT			**LOW DEVELOPMENT**		
101	China	.699	145	Kenya	.519
121	Indonesia	.629	146	Bangladesh	.515
131	Iraq	.590	149	Myanmar	.498
135	Ghana	.558	177	Sierra Leone	.359
136	India	.554	185	Mozambique	.327

Source: UN, Human Development Report, 2013

These issues matter. A workforce that has limited education and poor health care will not be an asset to employers. And if there are a few very rich people and many very poor people, there will be relatively small markets for most products. There is much more scope for businesses where there is a growing group of educated, healthy people, with middle incomes that are rising steadily. They will start by buying fridges and TVs, perhaps moving on to air conditioners if the climate is hot. They will also be providing tax revenues that allow governments to improve the infrastructure. This is part of JCB's story.

There is a hen and egg problem here. Weak infrastructure is very much a feature of low levels of development. It inhibits business growth because it raises the costs of communications and transport, among other things. This can go on for a long time because once economies begin to grow, it can be difficult for governments to keep up with the continuously growing need for better infrastructure. In particular, road building may prove slow, leading to serious traffic jams in the cities. Thailand has grown well over several decades but Bangkok is still seriously congested by any standards. For JCB of course, this creates opportunities rather than threats.

How stable is the government?

Political instability can make some markets very unattractive. While strong prospects of profit will still draw a business to invest even when the government is unstable, the risks will be greater. Oil companies typically brave some very delicate political situations, though they may try to avoid war zones. There is a trade-off between risk and profitability. Many businesses will seek to develop relationships with politicians in order to reduce the risks and of course some see corrupt practices as a way of enhancing their safety. You can see straight away that small or medium sized, less powerful businesses, will be greatly deterred by instability.

Is there a legal framework that will protect businesses?

The short answer to this question is, sometimes but not always. Many emerging economies have laws that enable businesses to go through the courts to collect bad debts. But in many other cases, the legal system works painfully slowly and is anyway unpredictable. It may not be easy to find well-qualified lawyers who can help. China has been slow to develop a reliable legal system and there is particular disquiet among US and other foreign businesses about piracy in the market place. This happens when competing producers make cheap, counterfeit copies of products that should be legally protected by trademarks and patents, i.e. by intellectual property rights (IPR).

The US government has tried hard to persuade the Chinese government to make legal action easier for foreign businesses and to strengthen its commercial laws. It is clear that the Chinese are trying to address the issues but many problems remain. Many other emerging economies have some similar problems. So an important aspect of the decision to invest will be a serious consideration of the risks associated with operating in a country where copying is widespread and access to legal redress may turn out to be limited.

Some emerging economies lack the legal system to protect trademarked products from piracy.

Are there problematic government policies?

Government controls can be a problem for foreign businesses. They know that all economies vary in certain respects and expect to have to fit in with local laws. The decision about where to locate will be affected by the extent of these constraints.

- How much tax will the business have to pay? Tax rates vary between countries, as to both the level and the way they are collected. Some big businesses will seek to arrange their affairs so as to minimise the profits made in high tax economies and maximise profits in low tax economies. Some countries where taxes are relatively low have been successful in attracting FDI, (for example, Ireland).

- Are there significant barriers to trade? Some governments try to exclude imports by taxing them or restricting the quantity. This is usually done in order to protect domestic producers from competition. (This is dealt with in Chapter 13 in more detail.) It can make some potential export markets rather unattractive.

- How difficult is it to start up a business? In the past, India had many bureaucratic controls that made setting up a business there very time consuming. Recent policies have made the process easier. Comparisons can be seen in Table 9.2.

- How favourable is the exchange rate? Exchange rates are often very flexible – and can be a source of great uncertainty. Selling exports in a foreign market that has an undervalued exchange rate can be quite a problem because of the competition. Domestic producers will have a price advantage. One solution would be to locate as much of the production process as is possible within the target market. The business may be able to cover its costs if much of its output is sold in the local market.

- Will there be government grants or subsidies available? In the EU, these are carefully regulated to ensure that the playing field is level, giving all member countries a chance to compete. Even so, there can be substantial help available in some areas.

Sizing up these and other considerations requires extensive research. When Nissan decided to locate a major car plant in the EU, it was looking to escape the EU's import duties. Years of negotiation preceded the decision to locate in Sunderland. The company liked the idea of being in an English speaking country and it established that suitably skilled labour would be available. But the grants offered by the EU and the UK and local governments were a key factor in the decision. These were designed to attract businesses into what had been a seriously depressed region for many years. More recently, many foreign businesses were attracted to Ireland by its combining the English language and the eurozone.

Table 9.2: Number of days required to start a business

Country	2008	2012
China	40	33
India	30	27
Malaysia	13	6
Mexico	28	9
Nigeria	31	34
Slovak Republic	16	16
United Kingdom	13	13
United States	6	6
World-wide average	38	30

Source: World Bank, Data Profiles

Car production in Slovakia

Slovakia emerged as a market economy after 1989, along with the rest of eastern Europe. By 1991, VW had taken over Skoda and was busily increasing efficiency. But by the mid-1990s Slovakia was still in the economic doldrums and the Slovak government decided to adopt business-friendly policies. It set up a new tax system with a flat tax of 19%. That meant that income tax, corporation tax, VAT and capital gains tax were all 19%. Businesses liked that – it was simple and predictable. In 2004, Slovakia joined the EU and soon after that it became clear that it was strong enough to join the eurozone

In 2003 PSA Peugeot-Citroen and KIA moved in and set up production lines. In 2006, 295,000 cars were produced in Slovakia, rising to 570,000 in 2007 and 927,000 in 2012. That made 171 cars produced per thousand inhabitants, the highest per capita level of car production in the world. (Slovakia has a population of 5.4 million.) The recession caused production to fall but growth resumed in 2010.

Slovakia abandoned the flat tax in 2013 – in favour of tax rates that rise with income. But the flat tax had done its job – making Slovakia look like a good place to do business.

Questions

1. What were the characteristics that attracted the car producers to Slovakia? Explain the importance of each one.

2. What potential risks would you expect them to consider?

Cultural and media issues

Businesses need to understand local cultures. Chapter 12 looks at the problems and pitfalls in more detail. Much more is known now about how to adapt to host countries' expectations and businesses can study the experiences of others who have gone before them in most parts of the world.

When JCB set up operations in India in 1979, they knew they were going into a country where many people spoke English, there were strong links between India and the UK and the country would be a good base for wider operations across Asia. They were helped by India's efforts to become more business-friendly.

Familiar methods of advertising may have to be replaced with media that are available and appropriate for the new market. This is an area where most businesses really need local help either from specialist local businesses or from able, skilled local people whom they can recruit directly.

The labour market

Planning for a new location includes finding out how easy it will be to recruit labour with appropriate skills for the technologies that will be used. It may be that training programmes are necessary and must be budgeted for. (Sources for all inputs must be identified, including any natural resources that are needed.) What will labour costs be? There may be a trade off between paying low wages and recruiting people with the necessary human capital – the issue that led Dyson to Malaysia. Wage costs will be an important element in determining the likely rate of return from the venture.

Corporate policy

Businesses vary as to the extent to which they want to expand abroad. For some, it is a matter of diversifying to reduce risks. LVMH found that growing sales in China gave it some protection from the 2008-09 recession in its western markets. JCB saw falling sales but then contained the situation because of its Asian markets.

Other businesses just become addicted to growth. One of their major objectives is to expand markets. If they have already expanded about as much as they can in the UK and face saturated markets, they may go on a shopping spree, looking for inorganic growth by buying up appropriate businesses abroad. Or they may set up their own factories or offices or retail outlets, growing organically wherever they feel confident of being able to create a market. A quick look at Tesco's operations outside the UK gives you a good idea of how it can work. Keep in mind that although Tesco is phenomenally successful, some of its overseas outlets have been a lot more profitable than others. (Why might this be?)

For some businesses expansion overseas is all about finding new sources of resources that they can exploit. Mining companies go to where the resources are and then export them to where there is a demand for them. BHP and Billiton both started out as tin miners, BHP in Australia (BH stands for Broken Hill, in New South Wales). Billiton was a Dutch firm that went tin mining in Indonesia. Both were well established by the end of the 19th century. Both got involved in other natural resources – e.g. oil and coal – and then in steelmaking, both with worldwide interests long before globalisation became the norm. They merged in 2001 and are now quoted on both the Australian and the London stock exchanges. The big new players in this field are now Chinese, seeking out raw material sources everywhere. High commodity prices give businesses a big incentive to seek out new sources.

For many, expansion overseas has two objectives, new markets, yes, but importantly, new locations for production, where costs will be lower. Much of the world's output of electronic chips comes from the Far East. Korea has long had an advantage in this field, starting out with cheap labour in the 1980s. Then as Korea prospered, wages rose and many manufacturers expanded into south east Asia where wages were lower. Now, Intel is thinking of locating its new plant in Korea, partly because it is close to China (where many of the chips will be assembled into consumer products) but very importantly because Korea has the appropriately skilled labour that they need. Similarly Dyson is doing well producing in Malaysia, where wages are far from being the lowest but scarce skills are available.

This illustrates the importance for businesses of being nimble. They need to make very careful cost comparisons and be very much aware of the trade-off between low-cost labour and quality human capital. Above all they need to be responsive to changes, not just in the markets where they sell but also in the labour markets and the commodity markets where they buy their inputs. Good access to information is really critical. Both moving into new markets and relocating production often make sense, but only if carried out with great care and detailed feasibility studies.

Chapter 10

Comparative and competitive advantages

A very technical product

Strix started out making control mechanisms in the Isle of Man in 1982. It was always an innovative business. It had a lot to do with the introduction of cordless kettles. Now it manufactures the tiny kettle sensors that monitor the temperature of the water inside and tell the kettle to switch off when the water is boiling. The sensor protects against boiling dry and contributes to the safety of appliances to which it is fitted.

In 2009 Strix celebrated the sale of its 1 billionth sensor. CEO Paul Hussey said success came from the company's "relentless pursuit of innovation, embedded in its culture, a combination that would see the wider application of the company's skills leading to Strix being defined as a global consumer technology solutions provider." He went on, "We're not resting on our laurels. At Strix there is a constant flow of innovation and we're always seeking new opportunities and global partners." One in five people in the world use Strix safety controls every day. The business has about two thirds of the world market in kettle sensors. Sales in 2009 were worth £85 million.

750 people are employed worldwide. The really technical part of the production process happens close to the head office in Ronaldsway, Isle of Man. These components are then shipped out to Guangzhou in China for assembly, along with other parts.

Strix is part of a trend whereby some small businesses specialise in highly technical devices that are usually hidden inside much larger products, greatly improving their functionality. Intel is the biggest example, manufacturing micro-chips. There are many others and most you will never have heard of.

Strix attributes its success to the very high quality of the people and the teamwork in its multicultural workforce. It recruits its design engineers and its production managers with the greatest care. But it also pays a lot of attention to the quality of its marketing and customer service teams. The CEO goes on: "We have forged lasting relationships with our valued partners around the globe, and continue to build and strengthen these links as we retain our market-leading position."

Questions

1. Why does it make sense to specialise in designing and manufacturing a small range of tiny products that consumers never see?

2. What is it about Strix that has enabled it to develop such a large market?

Specialisation

What happens when people get together to produce something? They don't all do the same things, each starting from scratch and producing a finished product. There is a **division of labour**. Each individual plays a part in the production process. With practice, each gets better at their own task. In the jam factory, some people supervise the boiling of the fruit and sugar, some arrange the process of putting it into jars and some are involved in putting on labels and lids and packaging in cartons. When there are economies of scale, the **specialisation** process goes further. There will be other specialists around, doing the accounts and the marketing. This saves a lot of time and allows small teams to achieve high output levels.

> **Division of labour** involves organising employees so that individuals specialise in one part of the production process. As they become quicker and more proficient at specific tasks, output increases.

> **Specialisation** means that people make the most of their skills by concentrating on what they do best. As a skilled person produces more, output per head rises. This only works when people or economies are in a position to trade their output for things they need but do not produce.

When you start to think about international trade, you see at once that economies become specialised, each producing the things they are best placed to produce. Their advantages may include natural resources, abundant land, cheap labour, scarce skills, technical know-how, a favourable climate, beautiful scenery, a deep-water port, a university active in scientific research or accessible sources of finance.

Absolute advantage

The USA clearly has an advantage in producing computers, compared to a country like Nigeria. This advantage is defined in terms of resources. One country will have an **absolute advantage** over another if it can create a product using fewer resources. Then it pays to specialise, producing more of the products in which the country has an advantage, and trade it for other things that are best produced elsewhere.

> An **absolute advantage** exists if the real resource cost of a product is lower in one country than another.

How much land, labour and capital does it take to produce bananas in the UK? Rather a lot, because we would be very inefficient producers of tropical fruit. Our resources would be much better used producing aircraft wings or kettle sensors. With bananas we would have to build and heat glasshouses. Large quantities of resources would be tied up in inefficient production. The Windward Islands have an absolute advantage in bananas, as do a number of other tropical countries. However, economies can still gain from trade even when they do not have an absolute advantage.

Comparative advantage

It is possible to show that specialisation and trade can almost always increase real incomes, using **the theory of comparative advantage**. This works even if one country has an absolute advantage in both the products being traded. (To keep this idea simple, we assume that there are two countries and two products.)

> **The theory of comparative advantage** states that if two countries each specialise in the product with the lowest opportunity cost, and then trade, real incomes will increase for both countries.

Comparative advantage relates to the opportunity cost of production. Provided opportunity cost structures differ between countries, every country will have a product for which its opportunity cost is lower than that of other countries. This is the product it can produce relatively more efficiently and in which it should specialise.

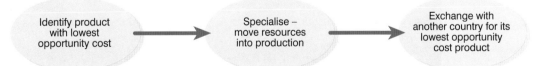

David Ricardo (1772–1823) earned a fortune as a dealer in the money markets. He then retired and set out to write about his ideas on economics. Comparative advantage was his most far-reaching idea. He used the example of Britain and Portugal, producing wine and cloth. Table 10.1 shows how the theory works.

The output shown refers to the amount obtainable from one unit of resources in each country. It is clear that Portugal is better at producing both wine and cloth. Nevertheless, Britain has a comparative advantage

in the production of cloth, because there the opportunity cost of cloth is one and half units of wine, as against Portugal's opportunity cost of two units of wine. Portugal has a comparative disadvantage in cloth. If Portugal specialises in wine and Britain in cloth, both will be better off.

Table 10.1: The theory of comparative advantage

Country	Output of goods		Opportunity cost ratio	
	Wine	Cloth	Wine	Cloth
Britain	60	40	$^2/_3$	$1^1/_2$
Portugal	90	45	$^1/_2$	2

How much better off?

Table 10.2 assumes that before trade, both countries split their resources evenly between production of the two products. After trade, both use all their resources to produce the product which has the lower opportunity cost. So long as the two countries have different opportunity costs, they will produce more if they specialise and trade.

Table 10.2: The outcome of specialisation

Country	Output of goods before specialisation		Output of goods after specialisation	
	Wine	Cloth	Wine	Cloth
Britain (10 units)	300	200	0	400
Portugal (8 units)	360	180	720	0
Total output	660	380	720	400

Portugal has a comparative advantage in wine production.

Ricardo's model is very simple. It assumes that transport costs are insignificant and that resources are mobile and can be relocated. But his thinking has had a profound influence because in fact, rising global exports have always led to rising global output. (See Figure 1, page 2 in the Introduction.) Exporting more raises GDP. Higher incomes mean people can afford more imports, which creates new markets for other producers. The link between trade and growth overall is well established, although it is always possible to find specific situations in which trade causes problems. This does not alter the fundamental conclusion.

Resources

Some countries are rich in natural resources, e.g. the USA. Others, e.g. Japan, have few natural resources but an educated, skilled labour force. Some have accumulated much highly productive capital – this applies to all developed countries. Some countries have knowledge of technologies that others do not have – this applies to the UK, among others.

Different products require different kinds of resources in different proportions. In aircraft production, the most important items are design, engineering and management skills and capital. The countries with the lowest opportunity costs in aircraft production will have all of these in abundance. Similarly, countries with a concentration of skilled computer programmers will produce software efficiently. Comparative advantage applies just as much to services as it does to goods.

Cheap labour can be crucial. Countries with low labour costs can sometimes produce manufactures with a low opportunity cost. But cheap labour is not the only factor. Other inputs may have a high opportunity cost. What matters is the overall opportunity cost. This makes it possible for the UK to continue to export high-quality knitwear, even though it does not have a comparative advantage in clothing generally.

Competitive advantage

The theory of comparative advantage is rather good at explaining why countries trade in order to obtain more goods and services. It shows quite clearly why some countries specialise in banana production while others produce and trade scientific instruments. But can it explain why some countries trade office equipment with each other, as the USA and the UK do? A large part of the growth of trade that has taken place over the past 50 years has come from countries swapping manufactured goods with each other.

For manufactured goods, design and technology have become very important in achieving competitiveness. Often, it is not the country that has an advantage in producing a specific product, but a particular business. It is this business that develops new products and efficient management techniques, rather than the economy as a whole, although education can help. In this situation it is more appropriate to think of businesses having a competitive advantage. It may compete on price or quality or after-sales service. Whichever it is, the business will grow.

The theory of comparative advantage works regardless of the level of the exchange rate. At any exchange rate, it still pays to trade because output increases. However, the exchange rate will affect who actually gets the increased output. A high exchange rate gives an economy a chance to buy more imports and can raise standards of living. A low exchange rate brings success in increasing exports and creates jobs. Exchange rates have an impact on competitiveness and can affect the pattern of trade.

Exploiting comparative advantages – the EU

The idea behind the EU is to promote free trade within Europe. Member countries get to buy from the most efficient supplier within the EU. Consumers have access to goods that are produced most cheaply and their real incomes can buy more. Since the UK joined the EU, trade with member countries has grown enormously.

- Before membership in 1973, about 30% of UK trade was with EU countries.

- By 1990, this had grown to 53% of trade and by 2007, 57%.

Many more UK businesses have got involved in this trade. There has been a real shift in the UK trade pattern. Traditionally, the USA was the UK's biggest trading partner. On a very simple level, more trade within the EU has increased consumer choice. It has intensified competition and brought some prices down, raising real incomes. It has provided many businesses with a larger market and helped them to exploit potential economies of scale. UK trade is not quite so closely tied to the EU as it was in 2007, because of falling demand in some of the eurozone economies in recent years. But the EU is still by far the UK's largest market.

Questions

1. How can the EU help member countries to exploit their comparative advantages?

2. Why might exploiting a comparative advantage increase real incomes?

3. Which countries have a comparative advantage in tourism? Why?

4. How is comparative advantage shifting in car production?

5. Does France still have a comparative advantage in fine wines? Why?

Does comparative advantage always work?

Australia and the UK both produced 13 million tons of wheat in 2007. But actually, Australia is a highly efficient producer of wheat and has a substantial comparative advantage. It has large areas of flat land that is ideally suited to growing crops and crop yields are high. It has a population little more than one third the size of the UK's. So whereas UK wheat production is for the domestic market, and will be supplemented by imports, Australia exports a large part of its wheat output at prices well below wheat prices in the UK.

So why don't we just save money and buy our wheat from Australia? Well, the answer lies in the Common Agricultural Policy of the EU. This places import controls on imports of agricultural products, so that EU farmers can make a profit even though for many products they do not have a comparative advantage. We could all have much cheaper food if it was traded freely.

Of course there is a food security argument for this – we have to be sure that we can feed ourselves in the event of war. Well, that's the argument, even though no war has disrupted global trade seriously since 1945. But there is another argument. We have to support our farmers so that their way of life is preserved and the countryside is used in the way it has been traditionally. (Do we? You could have a good debate about this. Which is more important, picturesque farms, the rights of farmers to carry on producing, or access to cheap food for people who want to eat economically?)

Anyway, in the EU we support farm incomes by controlling food imports. It drives the Australians mad and a good many other food exporters too. There is more on trade barriers generally in Chapter 13. UK trade is not quite so closely tied to the EU as it was in 2007, because of falling demand in some of the eurozone economies in recent years. But the EU is still by far the UK's largest market.

Chapter 11

Corporate social responsibility on the global level

First Quantum Minerals

First Quantum Minerals is a mining and metals company engaged in mineral exploration, development and mining. The Company which operates in Africa and Europe, produces copper and copper products, and gold. First Quantum has a strong policy based on corporate social responsibility (CSR). Some of its activities are listed below.

Kanshansi

Kanshansi is a copper mine in Zambia. Some of the projects undertaken so far include the drilling and equipping of water bores to supply clean water to villages and communities surrounding the mining area; resurfacing of the Solwezi town market; repairs to the town's infrastructure including bridges and roads; and repairs to the mortuary at Solwezi General Hospital. In an effort to reduce deforestation in the local area, Kansanshi has promoted alternative livelihoods in the area including beekeeping.

Guelb

Guelb Moghrein is a gold and copper mine in Mauretania. The company has focused on:

- the refurbishment of schools in the nearby town of Akjoujt

- repairs to medical facilities, construction of shade houses to grow vegetables for the local community

- assistance to local farming cooperatives in the form of water pumps and pipes to enable irrigation and improve the production of vegetables from garden plots

- the provision of water bladders in parts of the town where there is no piped water system

- the supply of clean water at no cost to low income families living along the 113 kilometre long Bennichab pipeline.

Zambia

First Quantum knows that a sustainable, fit, healthy workforce is essential for the company to achieve its business objectives. It runs an HIV/Aids programme at its three Zambian mines. The Zambian HIV prevalence rate is approximately 16% of the population. The company provides considerable support in terms of counselling, free medical care including treatment of opportunistic infections, and antiretroviral treatment for all employees and their families.

Questions

1. Why might First Quantum have adopted a CSR policy?

2. Assess the extent of the trade-off between a CSR policy and profits for First quantum.

Corporate Social Responsibility has become more and more important in recent years. There is some controversy over the reasons for the rise of CSR. Supporters of CSR would argue that businesses have much to gain and that they benefit in multiple ways by operating with a wider outlook than their own immediate, short-term profits. Others simply say it is the 'right thing to do' and that altruism is part of modern business practice. Critics argue that CSR conflicts with the fundamental economic role of the business, which is to make a profit; others argue that it is nothing more than cynical 'window dressing' to placate hostile public opinion or to pre-empt the role of governments as watchdogs over powerful businesses.

> **Corporate social responsibility** has been defined as "How companies manage the business processes to produce an overall positive impact on society." The World Business Council for Sustainable Development used the following definition: "Corporate Social Responsibility is the continuing commitment by business to behave ethically and contribute to economic development while improving the quality of life of the workforce and their families as well as of the local community and society at large."

Whatever the reasons, many local communities have benefited from CSR. It can take the form of investment in the local community, as in the case of First Quantum Minerals. Or it may be in the form of direct help, such as Google's commitment to contribute resources, as well as employee time, to address some of the world's most urgent problems. 1% of Google's equity and profit is donated to appropriate projects by Google.org. So far it has committed over $100 million in grants and investments to a wide range of projects ranging from research into environmental problems to global health programmes. Possibly Google hopes this generosity will make us more tolerant of its tax avoidance policies.

Having a CSR policy does not mean that a company is necessarily squeaky clean. In the USA a giant energy company gave millions to local charities and was forever winning national awards for its CSR work. The business was called Enron, and it collapsed in 2001 with debts of $31.8bn (£18bn), after it was revealed that its boss had orchestrated a giant fraud. It is also perhaps hard to accept the claims of the giant tobacco companies to be socially responsible.

Shareholder value

The traditional perception of business is that shareholders' interests are paramount. After all, they own the business. Everything that managers do should be directed towards the best interests of the shareholders. If shareholders want short-run profit maximisation at the expense of long-term growth, then it is the responsibility of business managers to deliver. Managers are employed to manage, on behalf of the shareholders. The needs, desires and aspirations of other interest groups should not take precedence over shareholder interests. This is the shareholder value view.

Many business experts condemn British managers for their preoccupation with short-run profits. They argue that merger mania and the desire to maximise shareholder value (which may come from profits or share price rises) are often not in the long term best interests of shareholders. Still less are they in the interests of other stakeholders. These attitudes are sometimes described as short-termism.

The stakeholder approach

The decisions that businesses make actually impact upon diverse groups of individuals, often referred to as **stakeholders**. These groups have their own objectives, which may or may not be compatible with those of the business as a whole, or with those of other stakeholder groups. Business decision takers have to balance these competing objectives.

> **Stakeholders** are all those people who have a 'stake' in a particular business. Stakeholder groups include customers, employees, suppliers, shareholders, creditors and local communities which are affected by the decisions of that business. Corporate social responsibility requires that the business recognises obligations to all these groups. Sometimes the environment is referred to as a stakeholder as well.

In contrast to the shareholder value view, the stakeholder approach to business decision making involves recognising that managers have a responsibility to take account of the interests of all the stakeholder groups that are affected. They must apply the principles of CSR to all stakeholders. It is often argued that the business will benefit significantly from the development of a co-operative approach. The benefits might include:

- Improved retention and motivation of staff.

- Closer relationships with suppliers, leading to better quality service.

- A reduction in the disruption of commercial activities by pressure groups.

- Improved public relations, resulting in more favourable media coverage, enhancing reputation.

Underlying these perceived benefits of the stakeholder approach, there is always a hope that by improving the reputation of the business, co-operative measures will actually lead to increased sales and sales revenue. So it is sometimes argued that CSR, as well as being morally right, is also good business practice and good for profits. So the motives for adopting CSR policies are often open to question.

Daimler

In Brazil, Daimler helped local residents to make auto parts from coconut fibres that were once discarded as waste. The result: a virtuous cycle that pays poor families a living wage, helps save the rainforest, and produces eco-friendly car components such as headrests and sun visors that can be recycled.

In the early 1990s, the University of the State of Pará in Belém in the north of Brazil launched the POEMA project (Poverty and Environment in Amazonia). The idea was to reforest rainforest areas, which had fallen victim to the 'slash-and-burn' approach, to restore them to their original condition and to create a new foundation for living for the local people.

Daimler initially committed $1.4 million to help start the project. Later they provided US$4 million to fund imported machinery and training in the use of the equipment. The result is a modern plant that has a production capacity of 80,000 tons/month. A total of 25% of its production is dedicated to demand for interior car parts at Daimler. The rest is for customers in the automotive industry such as General Motors and Honda. The plant is adding other product lines such as gardening pots and mattresses.

This is not just some philanthropic idea to make Daimler look good. It makes sound economic sense for the company, which saves on production costs and improves its environmental credentials. The rural communities benefit as well by supplying the coconut fibre. This has created approximately 4,000 new jobs including agricultural producers and processing plant workers.

Questions

1. In what ways might Daimler benefit from the policies described above?

2. What kinds of pressures may have induced the company to adopt such policies?

Stakeholders vs. shareholders

Many businesses have adopted the stakeholder approach. Some have encountered resistance from shareholders worried about the impact of this on profits, share prices and dividends. Meantime expectations placed on business have grown and pressure groups have become more vociferous. Activists may buy a single share in a company which they believe is acting against the interests of the community. This gives them the right to attend Annual General Meetings and if their interventions are carefully thought out, they can have considerable impact.

In reality it may be impossible to satisfy the demands of all stakeholders. The management must attempt to prioritise competing demands, and there will be opportunity costs and trade-offs. Inevitably, questions arise as to whether CSR has become a public relations exercise rather than an ethical basis for decision making. Figure 11.1 shows the diverse pressures on businesses, all of which may be opposing the shareholders. The orange-shaded groups often have close links to the media and the impact of adverse publicity can be devastating to business reputations.

Figure 11.1: Stakeholder pressures

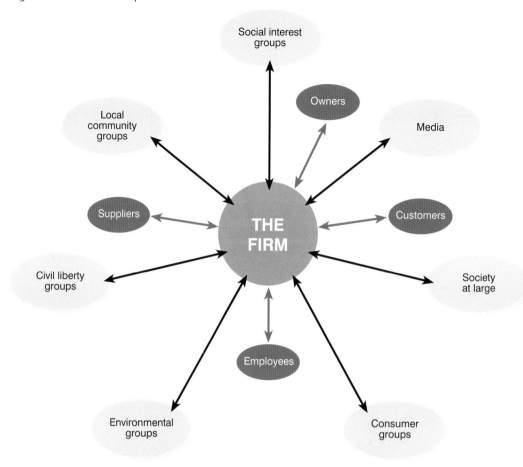

The decisions that may be affected

Many decisions have an ethical dimension, especially when they are being made on a global basis.

- Environmental factors are an obvious example, as with First Quantum Minerals and Daimler. Mining by its nature tends to have negative environmental effects. Big businesses generally will often take over significant amounts of land, which may displace local agricultural activities. In both cases, spending money on local environmental projects can help to offset some of the costs of development, and make the resulting economic growth a little more sustainable. Offering jobs to local people can help too, provided they actually end up with an improving standard of living.

- Some activities involve locating in places that would be best left undeveloped, if the interests of local people were the paramount consideration. Building dams and setting up palm oil plantations, as well as mining, can be highly destructive of communities as well as the environment.

- Where should the marketing effort be concentrated? Tobacco companies face falling sales in the developed world so have targeted developing countries, especially China. Is this right?

- How labour or capital intensive should production be? Many governments are more concerned about creating jobs than facilitating capital intensive production, which may not always benefit poorer people. Some businesses are inclined to invest in labour-saving capital as a way of reducing the cost of training and managing the workforce, just to avoid hassle. Labour intensive production could cost less.

- Pay and working conditions also figure large in debates about business responsibility. Many businesses outsource production in order to benefit from lower wage costs. They may also hope to cut costs by moving production to a location where laws on working conditions are less stringent. The case study below on Foxconn shows how serious this can be. This is discussed further in Chapter 17.

Foxconn and Chinese employees

Foxconn is the world's biggest electronics contract manufacturer. The company is based in Taiwan but much of its production takes place at a huge factory town near Shenzhen in south China. 90% of the 300,000 workers live in dormitories and earn low wages. The customers include Sony, Dell, Hewlett Packard, Motorola and Apple. Working conditions at Foxconn are not especially harsh by local standards, though they are not at all pleasant. There are always people who are keen to find employment there – people who hope to leave the countryside where wages are very low indeed and employment is often intermittent.

In 2010 a spate of suicides drew attention to pay and conditions at Foxconn. The company felt sure that in each case, there were emotional reasons for the suicides. But they were widely reported in the media. An experienced ex-employee of Foxconn said "Our generation has a broader horizon, more access to information than our parents. The most important thing for us is to realise our values in life, not just endure." Others have pointed out that new entrants to the labour market have often come from more urban backgrounds and, born after the start of the one-child policy, they have been treasured only-children. They aren't as tough as the older migrant workers were.

In other words, Chinese employees have more aspirations than they used to have. They want better working conditions and more pay. Trade union activity is still strictly controlled in China and strikes can be severely punished. But the suicides rattled Foxconn. They quickly announced a 30% pay rise for 2010 and some competing companies began to follow suit. Some of Foxconn's customers expressed anxieties about rising costs.

Questions

1. Explain three reasons why Foxconn might have considered a pay rise even if the suicides hadn't become a problem.

2. Evaluate the likely impact of rising wages in China.

Is ethical decision making just another kind of CSR?

Ethical business involves basing decisions on a set of clearly defined moral principles, and striving to do the right thing regardless of purely commercial considerations. Obviously this includes many elements of CSR – recognising obligations to stakeholders. But it goes beyond that in a deliberate attempt to operate on the basis of declared moral values.

> **Ethical decision making** means following codes of practice that embody moral values. The objective is to do the right thing, acting with honesty and integrity and taking into consideration the interests of everyone affected by the decision.

Within each business there are individual managers who have personal values and moral codes, which influence their decisions. In some businesses there is also a corporate culture, deliberately devised to embody a consensus view of how the business should be run and setting out key principles that are relevant to the company's activities. Clearly the outcome depends on the precise nature of the moral values that are adopted.

Early examples of ethical businesses were The Body Shop and Ben and Jerry's Ice cream. Google followed with its well-known slogan 'Do No Harm'. Google found it quite difficult to defend some of its decisions as the firm grew and issues multiplied. Nevertheless the view that businesses should behave in an ethical manner has gained ground, especially with some consumers. The idea of Fair Trade – paying a fair price for the products bought – is just one part of this trend.

Business in developed countries can relocate to a developing country and export their pollution.

While there is a lot of overlap between CSR and ethical decision making, the latter goes some way beyond CSR. The stakeholder approach involves considering the interests of stakeholders, but ethical business goes further in using moral values as a basis for a consistent approach, based on what is right.

CSR may go no further than scrupulously observing the law in the country of operation. Ethical decisions would recognise that the law may not necessarily protect the interests of all stakeholders. Therefore the business must set its own standards because it would be wrong to take advantage of a lax legal framework, for example by exploiting employees whose bargaining power is weak.

CSR in some businesses can mean looking after all stakeholders because that is actually the most profitable strategy for the long run. It is perfectly possible for businesses to adopt an ethical stance for the same reasons, perhaps because it is likely to be popular with consumers. In that case, the public relations information really does have to stand up to close scrutiny.

If the supposedly ethical business has blown its own trumpet, publicised its ethical decisions and concealed aspects of its activity that are plainly not ethical by widely held standards, then its clear lack of integrity will do a great deal of damage. The bankers, Goldman Sachs, claimed to put their clients first at all times. When it was found that they had knowingly sold them financial products without explaining the risks accurately, and made a good deal of money in so doing, they lost much of their reputation overnight. The shareholders and the employees, of course, were not unhappy. But many customers were dismayed.

The role of social audits

Social audits allow businesses to measure their progress towards responsible decision-taking. They recognise the responsibility of the business to provide information and the rights of the public to know about the social and environmental impact of its commercial activities. The audit process allows the values and expectations of employees to be considered alongside those of shareholders and the community generally. Communication between stakeholders is encouraged and trust and mutual respect may develop.

> **Social audits** highlight the progress, or lack of it, of a business that is committed to acting responsibly towards all its stakeholders.

Social audits are the outcome of what is often called social accounting, or social, ethical and environmental accounting. To be effective, there must be a clearly defined corporate vision, with well-publicised aims and objectives and well-defined corporate values. Businesses that have used this approach include BT, Shell, BP and the Co-op Bank. Many small organisations in the not-for-profit sector also produce some kind of social account.

For some companies, a social audit would be seen as something that might be very difficult to live up to. Exposing the true costs of their activities would mean committing themselves to do something about them and that might affect profits. Also, some organisations may find that their core values are superior to those of some of their stakeholders. A social audit only works when there are regular and effective two-way communications between stakeholders. On the other hand, the business that comes under fire from the public about, say, conditions in its overseas suppliers' factories (as Nike did) may need to clean up its act in order not to lose large numbers of customers. A social audit is a good way to demonstrate that some improvement has taken place (if it really has).

Ethics and the environment

In developed countries, there are many legal restrictions on business activities that degrade the environment. Businesses in developing countries are typically less regulated. One way for businesses in developed countries to get around the costs of cleaning up their production processes is to relocate to a developing country. They simply 'export' the polluting activity. This is one reason why greenhouse gas emissions are growing faster in developing countries now.

It is clear that this is not an ethical way to care for the environment. But developing countries compete for foreign investors and their poorly paid people want the jobs. Very difficult issues arise when nations and communities are faced with pressing needs to deal with both poverty and pollution. These play out in difficult international negotiations that often end in failure to agree – as happened at the UN climate Conference in Copenhagen in late 2009.

At Copenhagen, the USA and others blamed developing countries for refusing to accept many of the proposed curbs on greenhouse gas emissions. The developing countries collectively blamed the developed countries, still the biggest emitters in terms of per capita quantities, for not doing enough to clean up the mess that they created. The widespread belief that climate change is not in fact caused by man-made developments makes it quite difficult for the biggest emitters to enact stricter environmental policies.

Some businesses aren't waiting for the law to change, but trying to reduce their environmental impact anyway as an ethical policy. But many others are carrying on business as usual. Similarly some countries are changing the law without waiting for international agreement. But ethical policies are still a minority enthusiasm. Disagreement about the size of the risks involved in climate change is a serious problem.

Discussion point

Think of three businesses that have CSR policies. Consider and discuss how effective these policies actually are. Do any of the three businesses have other motives for pursuing their CSR policies, besides providing benefits for people affected by their business decisions? You might choose to use the case study on page 61 as one of your examples.

Chapter 12

Why do social and cultural differences matter?

A big mistake at Whirlpool

Whirlpool, the white goods manufacturer, wanted to produce a 'World Washer'. It would be a single, standardised model, designed to suit a wide range of markets and simple enough to be priced competitively and sell to people on middle incomes in developing countries. It was launched in Brazil, Mexico, China and India. The machine sold well – except in India. Whirlpool had invested heavily in distribution systems, designed to reach a potentially huge but geographically fragmented market. It sent a team to India to find out what had gone wrong.

The team discovered that many traditional Indian garments are made from fine silk or cotton. They were getting caught in a one millimetre gap around the edge of the drum. Whirlpool redesigned the machine to suit the Indian market. Eventually it recouped its losses but that took many years.

Whirlpool had assumed that all its target markets were much the same. The designers of the World Washer did not know about clothing styles in India.

Questions

1. Why do many firms make mistakes when they look to sell their products in new markets?

2. Suggest two ways in which Whirlpool might have avoided this mistake and show how they might have worked.

Social and cultural differences can be very significant. They have to be taken into account in any activity that involves collaboration between different groups of people. Their impact is easily under-estimated! From inside our own culture, we might imagine that all human beings have similar aspirations and expectations. We would be quite wrong.

The term 'culture' refers to the shared attitudes, values, customs and expectations that define groups of people. Social differences come into play when different groups of people have different ways of communicating and different expectations about the way people customarily behave. Values are the principles that guide people in their relations with each other. We can talk about cultural differences between societies, nations or economies. But we might also talk about differences between groups that can be identified within individual nation states. These are the basis for market segments.

In business we speak of **corporate culture**, which may include an expectation that people will be flexible. But in fact some are very inflexible, because they take decisions about product design and marketing that suit their own existing objectives. If firms with inflexible business models start to expand abroad, they can encounter difficulties. Unfamiliar national and local cultures can confound their expectations about the markets in which they propose to operate. They may also find that the people with whom they want to do business have unfamiliar habits and conventions. If they are to communicate effectively with potential partners, they will have to respect local patterns of behaviour.

> **Social and cultural differences** come from the fact that individual societies and groups within them may have a distinctive way of life. This will affect their patterns of consumption and the products they favour. But it will also affect the way they do business with one another.
>
> **Corporate culture** – the set of important assumptions that are shared by people working in a particular business and influence the ways in which decisions are taken there.

Areas of difference

Whirlpool ran into difficulties when it started to design new products for different countries. The basic rule here is never simply to assume that if customers in one country like the product, customers in other countries will too. Product design can be crucial in determining whether it sells well and detailed knowledge of the market in question is needed to ensure that designs are appropriate.

Equally important are differences in the way people communicate with each other. These can have many different effects. Obviously language barriers operate at every level. Businesses need bilingual people who can advise them on how to avoid the pitfalls. But there are many other sources of difficulty.

- Conventions in business discussions vary hugely and potential business partners have to be approached in ways that will not offend them. This means that people who are going to negotiate deals in culturally different economies have to be very well briefed so as to avoid possible misunderstandings.

- Differences in the way people communicate must also be explored before planning advertising campaigns and promotional activities.

- The marketing message itself will have to be set out in terms that are meaningful and appropriate to the culture in question. Literal translations of advertising slogans are particularly likely to fail. Brand names may need to be adapted.

Local pricing strategies may have to be devised and distribution systems must be appropriate too. In short, market orientation is even more important in international business than it is when selling in a domestic market. According to Deloitte, the big accounting and consultancy firm, fewer than half the businesses that have entered **emerging markets** in the past twenty years describe themselves as having been 'very successful'. Some fail altogether and some live in hope that their costly investments in new markets will eventually pay off.

> **Emerging markets** are usually defined as those that are not yet fully developed but have a group of middle class consumers that is large and prosperous enough to provide a market for developed country products.

What to do?

Whirlpool wasn't the only company that made mistakes as it sought out new markets. But stories like theirs get around. Action was taken. Deloitte's research shows that 40% of businesses that compete in emerging markets now get their products designed locally. Unilever, the giant manufacturer of food and household products, has set up 68 different innovation centres across 20 countries. They study local markets and devise the products that best meet their needs. Unilever's approach means that they can cater for different market segments or regions within countries.

Some businesses have assumed that if the customers have low incomes, prices must be kept low. Up to a point this is true – Levi Strauss couldn't sell its high priced jeans in India. It had to change its price and design strategy and came up with some affordable jeans, which sold well. But there is a saying in Latin America "what is cheap ends up being expensive". If low prices seem to imply low quality, some compromise has to be the answer.

Future Brands CEO Santosh Desai says "The usual approach is to strip the product of features until a semblance of affordability is attained. The trouble is that the emerging consumer, for whom every act of discretionary consumption is an act of sacrificing something essential, is looking to be seduced rather than patronised. Products must be appropriate, not just cheap."

Horses for courses

Nokia keeps full time design staff who do nothing but study the way consumers use their phones. They have produced phones with multiple phone books, to suit countries where, typically, several people will share a phone. They have made their phones dust resistant for very dry countries and now offer user interfaces in 80 different languages. They keep the price down by reducing the number of features, add-ons and apps that wealthier users appreciate. But they make sure that there are no compromises with design features that are important in ensuring reliability.

Mobile phones are spreading across Africa fast because they do not require expensive infrastructure, as land lines do. Whereas in developed country markets, there is a long history of innovation so that designers can be quite conventional, successful new products in emerging economies need a more radical approach. But this requires designers to be very sensitive to cultural norms in the market concerned.

Question

Find two more stories of successful product development for an emerging market. If you don't know where to begin, try researching the Freeplay Radio.

Appropriate marketing

When Pepsi first started to sell in the Chinese market, they used the slogan that was current at the time, 'Pepsi Brings you Back to Life'. The drink didn't sell well. Translated directly into Chinese, the slogan meant, 'Pepsi Brings Your Ancestors Back from the Grave'. Swift changes were made but such gaffes can be damaging for quite a while.

General Motors had a problem too, when they wanted to sell the Chevy Nova in Latin America. They realised why sales were disappointing when they discovered that in Spanish, 'nova' means 'it won't go'. When they renamed the car as the 'Caribe', sales improved rapidly.

Businesses that want to expand into new markets must allow time to get to know their target markets. They must seek out partners and decide whether a joint venture may be appropriate. They will need to find local agents and perhaps also hire local employees who have a good understanding of the relevant markets. They may decide to trial some products in a small area. All of these require up-front investment – and that is just to get the necessary market research in place. Only after that can the planning process move on to product design and marketing.

Danone and Wahaha

Joint ventures have helped many businesses to get into the Chinese market. So in 1996, Danone, the French food group, joined up with Wahaha, which is and was run by Zong Qinghou, whose story was very impressive. He worked for 15 years as a farm labourer and then got a job in a paper box factory. In 1986 he saw that the market-oriented reforms that the Chinese government had introduced would open up big possibilities for business. With a loan, he set up in business selling ice creams and nutritional supplements. His business grew fast and in 1996, when Danone was looking for a partner, Wahaha looked like the ideal joint venture (JV) candidate. Danone bought a 51% controlling interest in four of the ten Wahaha subsidiaries and set up a new distribution company, making a total of five joint ventures.

Danone had overall control at the board level and appointed a finance director, Stephen Yau. They also appointed an assistant for Mr Yau, a marketing director and and R&D director. Otherwise, Wahaha was entirely responsible for the day-to-day running of the five companies. The deal included various confidentiality and non-competition agreements, designed to ensure that Wahaha subsidiaries did not compete directly with Danone.

The joint ventures were successful and Mr Zong believed that this was entirely due to his efforts. The number of JV subsidiaries grew to 36. But Mr Zong went on creating new Wahaha subsidiaries as well – altogether 96 of them. Danone eventually decided that these Wahaha subsidiaries were competing directly with the JV products. The dispute grew and grew.

A Swedish arbitration tribunal decided in favour of Danone. Even so, Danone decided to settle with Mr Zong without further debate. They sold the JVs back to him for 21% less than their book value. Mr Zong said he had set up the new Wahaha subsidiaries because he had become frustrated with Danone's cautious approach to expansion. He said a major reason for the dispute was a clash of cultures. The deal took him 15 places up the China rich list, to number 3, with an estimated personal fortune of $4.8 billion. By 2012 he was China's richest man with US$20.1 billion.

Questions

1. Why would Danone have thought that its original agreement with Wahaha would be a success?

2. How might Mr Zong have argued that the success of the JV subsidiaries was all of his making?

3. What might have been done in the early stages to avoid misunderstandings?

The Asian Way

Although business conventions do differ from country to country, Asian countries do have some common features that call for a markedly different approach to that adopted in the West. Very importantly, Asians expect to spend time building trust between business partners. So the early stages of negotiating a joint venture in Asia would normally require a number of meetings, including lengthy meals out, to give everyone a chance to learn about each other and establish a degree of trust. Some businesses might think that these social occasions are a waste of time but this may not be so if the need to build trust is recognised.

There are numerous areas of difficulty and some are more important than others. Not speaking for too long at a time when using an interpreter makes sense. Holding a business card with both hands when presenting it is a simple way to observe the Asian custom. It is wise to avoid talking about sensitive political issues because being criticised or losing face is always very problematic for people from the Far East, especially China.

The key requirement is to spend time finding out how to behave without offending potential allies in the context of the relevant national culture. Body language can be just as, if not more important than speech. Gestures that are friendly in one culture may be anything but, in another. In the matter of building trust, quite small misunderstandings can prove to be setbacks. You may have seen HSBC adverts in airports giving information on differing meanings in different cultures. The idea is that businesses should use their briefing services. This confirms that preparing to enter a new market is usually more costly than exporters expect.

Adapting to change

Many businesses have made serious money by breaking into new markets. But many have found their new markets extremely risky. Some have withdrawn while others continue to pour money into their projects in the hope of long term gains. This is a situation in which potential rewards are high but risks are also significant.

Being well informed about cultural differences can reduce the risks. The most successful businesses are nimble – they can adapt to change by keeping themselves well informed and moving swiftly when the facts change. They are flexible enough to work within differing cultures and can take complex decisions based on accurate information. All this requires willingness to invest time and money in the planning process.

Chapter 13

What do trade barriers do?

Tyres and steel pipes

President Obama made promises to the American people during his 2008 electoral campaign. He said he would protect US jobs. Some of us wondered whether he meant this.

By autumn 2009, the recession was leading to redundancies. Trade unions in the tyre industry were complaining stridently about a surge in US imports of Chinese tyres, saying they had led to 7,000 job losses in US factories. President Obama imposed a new import duty of 35%, on top of the existing duty of 4%. The Chinese government was livid. Mr Chen, the minister of commerce, said "this is a grave act of trade protectionism. Not only does it violate WTO rules, it contravenes commitments the US government made at the G20 summit." The ministry said it would investigate imports of US poultry and vehicles.

The US responded in kind. "Retaliation would be inappropriate, as the US acted entirely within the bounds of trade laws and within the safeguard provision that China itself agreed to upon accession to the WTO." US officials said that if China retaliated, they would make a formal complaint to the WTO.

Questions

1. Assess the significance of the connection between international trade and economic growth.

2. Why does public opinion sometimes support the use of import controls?

3. Why do the governments of exporting countries retaliate when import controls are introduced?

4. Evaluate the effects that import controls are likely to have (a) in the short run and (b) in the long run.

5. Why might one think that President Obama did not really mean to increase barriers to trade, before he became president?

Why trade?

The whole point of trade is to get what you want from the supplier whose products provide the best value for money. Cheap imports are very pleasing – they make our incomes go further and often raise standards of living. When we can get the things we have to have at reasonable prices, we have more money left over to spend on other things. This can apply to services as well as goods – think of tickets for football matches, theatres and cinemas.

But when jobs and incomes are threatened, it is very tempting for governments to try to protect sectors that are vulnerable to competition from abroad. The obvious way to do this is to control imports. This can be done using **tariffs** or **quotas**, or a combination of measures.

Tariffs are taxes placed on specific imported goods. They are sometimes called import or customs duties.

Quotas are physical limits on the level of specific imports in any one year.

How tariffs work

When tariffs are levied in order to curb imports, the intention is usually to protect a domestic producer of a substitute. The substitute may or may not be a good one. But if it is, as with Chinese tyres in the US, then demand will be elastic, so when prices rise to cover the cost of the tariff, imports will fall substantially. The domestic producer will sell more and may be able to raise prices and increase profits. Figure 13.1 shows what happens.

Figure 13.1: Tariffs on products that have elastic demand

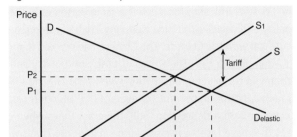

Tariffs can be used in a range of circumstances.

- They can be used to protect specific industries or sectors from foreign competition. Many developed countries want to protect their agricultural sectors. The EU's Common Agricultural Policy (CAP) protects farmers; for some products it is very restrictive indeed. For example cane sugar can be produced much more cheaply than sugar made from sugar beet. So sugar prices within the EU are often well above world prices. Higher prices for many food products mean that consumers' real incomes are reduced. On the other hand, farm incomes are high enough to keep farmers in business.

- Tariffs raise tax revenue: if demand for the relevant import is inelastic, people will continue to buy it even though the price is higher and the government will receive taxes that can be used to help fund public expenditure.

- Tariffs can be used to deter **dumping**. This occurs when the exporter is selling the product at a price lower than that at which they can sell in their home markets. Consumers are often pleased to be able to get very cheap imports but a firm that is competing with dumped imports will usually feel very aggrieved about it. This is what happened with the Chinese tyres sold on US markets in 2009. The WTO permits anti-dumping duties under certain circumstances, in order to deter unfair competition.

- The **infant industry** argument holds that if small industries, those that are just getting started, are protected for a while, they may in time become more expert and reap economies of scale, and so be able to compete effectively without protection. This is an argument for temporary measures.

> **Dumping** means exporting at a price that is less than the true cost of production.
>
> **Infant industries** are those with some prospect of profitability in the long run, provided they are given some protection in the short run while they get started.

When governments use import controls to protect many of their domestic producers, they are said to be adopting inward-looking policies. On the whole, these have not been successful except in isolated instances. The snag with import controls generally is that although they do reduce imports, they also annoy the exporter. If that leads to retaliation, it may mean that jobs are lost in exporting industries.

When tariffs cause prices to rise, demand may be inelastic (i.e. substitutes are either unavailable or inferior). That means that people will simply buy the imported item anyway and pay the higher price. This leaves them with less money to spend on other things. Tariffs on cars or video games may make domestic

manufacturers happy. But if they lead to people having less money to spend on meals out, restaurant owners and their employees will be unhappy.

There are two snags with tariffs, generally. One is that they cause a welfare loss (i.e. a loss of real income) to the consumer. Higher prices reduce purchasing power. The other is that when you cut down imports, you are reducing incomes in the exporting country. They will have less money to spend on imports – so your exports are going to fall too. Retaliation could further reduce exports.

President Obama knew this when he put tariffs on tyres. (He went on a few months later to put tariffs on steel pipes as well, to protect the US steel industry, for much the same reason as in the case of tyres.) He also knew that US exports of poultry and vehicles to China were tiny. He had worked out that these tariffs were not going to spark a real trade war with the Chinese. The Chinese had worked that out too. They knew that WTO rules permit some anti-dumping duties. The threat of tariffs on poultry and vehicles was a bit like threatening to tickle your enemy in the playground. Within weeks, the US and Chinese governments were talking amicably again. Trade is just too important for everyone. Protection can have very serious consequences and can turn a recession into a depression. Still, there are times when governments really want to help firms and employees that have faced a massive surge in imports. That's why the WTO allows some anti-dumping duties on a temporary basis. These can make the adjustment process easier.

Still, for a while in 2008 and early 2009, there were very real fears that protectionist pressures would lead to a repeat of the beggar-thy-neighbour policies of the 1930s. Although some countries introduced a few new tariffs, generally this did not happen.

How do quotas work?

Quotas set a physical limit on imports of individual products. If demand is at a low level anyway, they will make no difference. But if demand is high, as in Figure 13.2, the price will be pushed up above its free market equilibrium. Consumers will pay a higher price for a smaller quantity than they would prefer to buy.

Figure 13.2: The effect of quotas

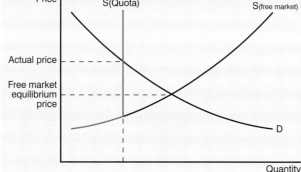

Exporters who are faced with quotas may in fact make increased profits from the higher prices they can charge when quantity is restricted. This will happen if there are few domestically produced competing products, i.e. good substitutes. The more inelastic demand is, the more the price is likely to rise when a quota is imposed. Quotas almost always inhibit competition, leading to inefficiency.

Other trade barriers

There are other kinds of protectionist policies, besides tariffs and quotas.

- Using subsidies to help a domestic industry can help it to compete. They may finance investment that raises productivity and cuts costs. Or they may simply allow the business to survive recession and continue in easier times. Government grants to US car producers in 2008-09 staved off imminent collapse but carried a requirement to restructure completely and close down uneconomic car plants. Both the US and the EU have subsidised Boeing and Airbus respectively, and both have complained about each other to the WTO.

- Keeping the exchange rate undervalued is a form of protection. In the past, the US government has accused China of manipulating its exchange rate to keep it low and strengthen Chinese exporters' competitiveness.

- Safety standards can be used to protect domestic industries. Nowadays they are most likely to be imposed in the food industry, where they may be thought to be necessary. However, some exporters complain that this is just hidden protectionism. There can be a fine line between safety and protection.

What can go wrong?

Any measure that restricts trade involves preventing some people from buying from the cheapest or best-value producer. So trade protection will always lead to falling real incomes in the long run. The problem is that industries do decline when competing imports become available and decline is painful. Some employees lose their jobs and the value of shareholders' investments will fall too. Both groups will lobby the government, seeking protectionist measures.

Businesses and people who suffer from competition can become very vocal and sometimes get popular support for their efforts to get protection. The trouble is, consumers of the relevant product are almost always more numerous than the people involved in producing it. But they are not an organised group. The following case study illustrates this. European footwear manufacturers are understandably annoyed about dumped shoes from China. But the people affected are few in number. The people who benefit from the cheap shoes – everyone in the EU who wears shoes, all half a billion of us – like to get them at bargain prices. The nub of the argument is that although import controls make some businesses more profitable, they reduce the profits of all those businesses that lose out because real incomes are lower.

Shoes and the EU

In 2005, EU markets were inundated with shoes imported from Asian markets, mainly China and Vietnam. EU figures showed that footwear imports from China had risen by 1000% since 2000. 1000 footwear manufacturers in the EU had closed down. The Mediterranean countries, especially Italy and Spain, which have for long had a comparative advantage in shoe-making, were putting on the pressure.

In 2006, the then EU Trade Commissioner, Peter Mandelson, who had a strong track record in opposing import controls, proposed a tariff of 20%, which he could justify under the WTO's anti-dumping rules. There was evidence of illegal state aid through tax breaks, non-commercial land sales and cheap finance, all of which would have helped Asian producers to sell at less than the full cost of production.

Clarks, the UK shoe giant, were appalled. They import vast quantities of shoes to sell in their retail outlets. "Twenty percent would be difficult to swallow," they said. "We will have to work very hard with suppliers and supply chains and profitability. To what extent consumer prices will have to rise and retail jobs will be lost – it is too early to comment but there will have to be some pain shared." Timberland joined Clarks in their criticisms.

EU members were divided. The southern members wanted protection. The northern members and the European Branded Footwear Coalition, an employers' organisation for footwear importers, whose members employ 17,000 people, argued against raising prices to consumers. In the end, tariffs of 16.5% on Chinese shoes and 10% on Vietnamese shoes were agreed, temporarily.

These tariffs were removed in 2011, partly because some EU shoe manufacturers wanted to expand their sales in China. The British Retail Consortium said the tariffs had on average added £1.60 to the price of every pair of imported shoes. They had cost British footwear consumers £330 million a year.

Questions

1. Explain the pros and cons of EU tariffs on imported footwear.

2. How were the tariffs justified by the EU trade commission? Why were they removed?

Outward-looking trade policies which reduced import controls, have led to faster economic growth.

The consequences of import controls

Trading partners get upset about import controls. The real problems arise if and when they decide to retaliate. Then the protectionist government has to watch its exports decline. So despite pressures from employers' organisations and trade unions whose members are suffering, most governments now resist wholesale import controls in favour of the rules-based system embodied in the WTO. You can see what has happened in the steady increase of the membership of WTO – very few countries are not either members or hoping to join before long.

It was not always so. Fifty years ago tariffs were far higher than they are now and there were many quotas. Some economies adopted **inward-looking trade policies**. The idea behind these is to protect domestic producers so that they can develop expertise, learn how to reap economies of scale and reduce reliance on expensive imports. This approach was used in India for several decades after independence.

> **Inward looking trade policies** use import controls to protect their domestic producers from foreign competition. Their aim is to develop their infant industries, which may eventually become strong enough to compete on world markets without protection.

Over time it became clear that outward-looking trade policies, which made trade freer by reducing import controls, led to faster economic growth. First the Asian Tigers and then China astonished the world with the speed of their growth. Governments that were doubtful about this approach came under pressure from the World Bank and the IMF.

The WTO held successive rounds of trade negotiations in which all member governments agreed to reduce tariffs and quotas. These dragged on for years and years but they did in the end achieve many of their objectives. This process of trade liberalisation was a big factor in globalisation. The latest round of WTO negotiations, the Doha Round, began in 2001 and stalled in 2008.

What can businesses do when faced with trade barriers?

If a business wants to export more, it must look at whether its exports will be subject to significant tariffs in each potential market, and whether there are other kinds of controls in place. Any import controls will affect sales levels and profitability. There may be an incentive to set up production within the country concerned – then the product won't be an import. Nissan and Toyota got around the EU's common external tariff by locating production in the UK.

Businesses lobby governments, representing the interests of employees and shareholders in whatever way they think may help. It is important to think carefully before deciding who is right – vested interests can make very strong cases that ignore the perspectives of other stakeholders (especially consumers).

Do you sometimes buy British in order to protect jobs in the UK?

How the WTO can help

The WTO researches trade issues, formulates rules and supervises trade negotiations which lead to agreements between member governments. Where import controls can be justified, the WTO favours tariffs and subsidies over quotas, because they distort competition less. It has strict rules about subsidies and tariffs. Where they are allowed, they are generally expected to be either low or temporary.

An important aspect of WTO membership is that governments can make formal complaints. There is a dispute resolution mechanism. This is particularly useful for complaints about dumping. It can be quite difficult to prove that dumping has happened. Information about producers' costs is not usually available. The importing country may try to levy anti-dumping duties. The exporter may protest that they are being penalised simply for being highly competitive. When this occurs, it helps that both parties can make use of the WTO dispute resolution mechanism. They get access to WTO experience of difficult issues. Individual businesses can take their complaints to their own governments which will take up strong cases on their behalf.

Despite the very serious recession since 2008, protectionism has not become a big problem. There have been government discussions in the G20 group and elsewhere and the general conclusion has been to avoid protecting a wide range of industries. There have been a number of new tariffs and subsidies but they have not reached a worrying level. As of 2013 there are concerns about solar panels but the Chinese government vigorously denies dumping. Some EU countries wanted to introduce anti-dumping measures but others did not. So far, Germany and many other EU governments remain convinced that protectionist measures would be a mistake. Given the dangers of retaliation, the cost of protection could be high.

Chapter 14

How do global industries develop?

There is a story about a BBC focus group set up to find out how far television audiences understand news reports. In one meeting, the then economics editor Evan Davies referred to "globalisation – whatever that means". A panelist replied: "Well if he doesn't know what it means, how the hell are we supposed to?"

Question

What do you think globalisation means?

The basic trends that produced the globalisation process were described in the first four chapters. But that process is very complex indeed and as you study it, more and more of the important aspects of it become understandable.

Globalisation is a much misunderstood term. For some it means a flawed economic model; the dominance of US and European corporate culture across the globe, with a Starbucks and McDonald's on every corner in every country. For some of its critics it is seen as a process by which rich western economies exploit less well endowed nations, with images of low-paid sweatshop workers symbolising all that is wrong with globalisation. Meetings of the WTO frequently used to attract protests from anti-globalisation supporters but these are now much less significant than they were.

Spectacular growth in Brazil is rooted in the steady growth of globalisation.

Others see globalisation as a positive force, bringing wealth and development to many countries. It has undoubtedly made billions around the world better off in both financial and material ways. The spectacular growth of economies like China, India, and Brazil is rooted in the steady growth of globalisation. It is also argued that it binds countries together and helps maintain peace and stability. Thomas Friedman, a Pulitzer prize-winning author, proposed the Golden Arches Theory, observing that no two countries with a McDonald's franchise had ever gone to war with one another. Sadly subsequent events in the Balkans and later in Georgia and Russia partially disproved this.

In essence, globalisation means the economic and commercial links and ties between countries worldwide. Numerous definitions – both economic and non-economic – of globalisation exist, but according to the International Monetary Fund (IMF), globalisation is "the process through which an increasingly free flow of ideas, people, goods, services and capital leads to the integration of economies and societies."

Globalisation is not a recent phenomenon; it is possible to trace waves of globalisation back to the 1800s. The period 1870-1913, for example, saw a significant increase in international trade, accompanied by cross-border flows of labour and capital. John Maynard Keynes remarked that in 1914, "The inhabitant of London could order by telephone, sipping his morning tea, the various products of the whole earth, and reasonably expect their early delivery upon his doorstep." It is interesting to speculate what the great man would have made of modern communication and delivery systems!

As a word, it has existed since the 1960s but came to prominence in the 1980s. In modern usage it has come to mean an ongoing and accelerating process of global integration and the breaking down of economic, social and cultural barriers between nations across the globe. In reality, the process of globalisation has been with us for as long as there has been trade between nations, but the main and modern thrust has been relatively recent since the 1980s. This chapter pulls the strands together and looks at how businesses have been affected by the global trends.

Global strategy versus global localisation

Some businesses succeed by having a global strategy that applies to all of their activities worldwide. This works well when their markets have similar expectations wherever they are. Oil and mining companies can do this. The cement manufacturers too – their product is used in construction everywhere. Locations may be based on where the raw materials are. A global approach to marketing may make good sense.

Where markets differ, the reverse holds. Businesses need to plan production and marketing strategies to fit cost differences between locations and individual market preferences. Solutions will vary hugely depending on the product and the market. The rest of this chapter provides a flavour of the many and various outcomes in individual businesses.

The rise of outsourcing

Over the last two decades, some highly populous, low-wage developing economies have emerged onto the world stage. China, India and others greatly increased their shares of global output, trade and foreign direct investment. They have undergone sweeping cultural, political and economic changes. Economic reforms in China in particular led to its accession to the WTO in 2001 and to ASEAN in 2010. (See Chapter 4, page 27 on ASEAN.)

At the same time these countries have seen an influx of FDI as many manufacturers closed down their plants in the US and Europe and relocated them, not just to China and India, but other countries such as Mexico, Brazil and many others. The reasons for this were discussed in earlier chapters. The attractions of these countries as low cost manufacturing bases, and sometimes also as potentially lucrative markets, have done much to speed the process of globalisation.

Increased liberalisation

With the collapse of the Berlin Wall in 1989, many previously restricted countries emerged blinking into the capitalist world; some such as the Czech Republic have forged ahead whilst others such as Romania have struggled by comparison. Elsewhere other countries have relaxed restrictive legislation, such as control over capital movements, regulation of financial markets and problematic labour laws. All of these trends reduce barriers to trade and encourage globalisation.

Increased harmonisation of laws

The creation of trading blocs has done much to encourage harmonisation of the many rules and regulations surrounding trade, making it much easier for countries to develop products that can access global markets. Elsewhere countries have been making efforts to align their laws in such areas as Intellectual Property Rights (IPR) and patents. The threat of not being able to protect your ideas and property in another country has been a considerable barrier to trade. China has made significant progress in this area, although there are still many complaints about pirate copying.

> **Intellectual Property Rights** (IPR) are the rights to own and to exploit ideas or inventions, of literary or other cultural works. Sometimes intellectual property rights are given a monetary value in financial statements, e.g. ownership of a patent to manufacture battery lawn mowers, or ownership of the score and text of a musical.

IPR in India

IPR protection or innovation was not widespread in India until recently. There were many reasons, e.g. little R&D investment, limited or no competition from foreign businesses, and archaic and difficult to navigate IPR laws. Customers had become used to the poor quality products and services being dished out on the pretext of 'self reliance' and 'made in India'. Overall, there was no market for innovation and no need for people to innovate.

This led to a culture where innovation was neither recognised nor rewarded. There was no incentive for companies to innovate or hire people who could innovate. Some of India's best and brightest people migrated to western countries where they could demonstrate their talent and creative skills.

The opening up of the Indian markets in 1991 and subsequent arrival of MNCs in India changed everything. The MNCs brought about a greater awareness of IPR and that forced the country and the government in particular, to start recognising IPR as an issue to consider. This led to India becoming a signatory to international treaties like the agreement on Trade-Related Aspects of Intellectual Property of the WTO. Since then India has been working to improve IPR protection and encourage more FDI but progress has been rather slow.

Questions

1. Why would the lack of IPR protection discourage innovation in India?

2. Why would it act as a barrier to entry?

3. Explain the likely impact on the Indian economy (a) before IPR protection was improved and (b) after.

The role of mergers and takeovers

There are two ways in which a business can grow and expand. **Organic growth** means that the business grows from within using its own resources; it does not take over other businesses but grows by investing and expanding output and sales from within. **Inorganic growth** occurs when a business gets bigger by joining with another firm. This can be achieved with a merger or a takeover. In some ways mergers and takeovers are similar, in that they combine two previously separate firms into a single legal entity. There is however, a difference. A **merger** involves the mutual decision of two companies to combine and become one entity; it can be seen as a decision made by two 'equals'. A **takeover**, or **acquisition**, on the other hand, is usually characterised by the purchase of a smaller company by a larger one. This does not necessarily have to be a mutual decision. A large company can initiate a hostile takeover of a smaller firm, which essentially amounts to buying the company in the face of resistance from the smaller company's management.

Many of our most familiar brand names have expanded by these means and their history can sometimes be seen in the name. GSK (GlaxoSmithKline) is the world's fourth largest pharmaceutical company and is a classic example of this:

- Glaxo laboratories + Boroughs Wellcome = Glaxo Wellcome

- Beechams + SmithKline Beckman = SmithKline Beecham

- Glaxo Wellcome + SmithKline Beecham = GlaxoSmithKline!! (Some steps were missed out too).

In 2009 the Volkswagen Group became the largest car producer in the world by volume (6,054,829 units for sale in 153 countries). It includes well known makes such as Audi, Seat, Skoda, Bentley and Bugatti. Altogether there are more than 350 companies operating within the group as a result of many mergers and takeovers. In 2012, VW sold over 9 million cars, even though it came second to Toyota.

Organic growth occurs when an individual business increases output. This type of expansion is likely to be quite slow but steady and secure.

Merger means combining with another company on a collaborative basis.

Takeover or **acquisition** refers to the situation where one company is buying another. This may be an amicable process or it may involve a hostile bid, which is not supported by the management of the business that is being taken over.

Inorganic growth occurs when a business expands by taking over or merging with another company. Both mergers and takeovers may allow rationalisation that can cut costs and expand markets. They may also yield economies of scale and a decrease in average costs.

The actual mechanics of how mergers and takeovers happen are relatively unimportant in this unit, but the impact of mergers and takeovers on global industries can be very significant indeed.

Heineken

In early 2010 Heineken, one of the world's largest brewers, launched a successful takeover of the Mexican group, Femsa Cerveza, which had 14 breweries in Mexico and Brazil. Among their brands were Sol and Dos Equis. It was almost exactly two years since Heineken, along with Carlsberg, had taken over Scottish & Newcastle breweries in the UK. Since then, the British beer market had declined, a combination of the smoking ban, the recession and a series of duty increases doing much to reduce trade. Heineken found it tough going.

The €5.3 billion (£4.8 billion) takeover of Femsa Cerveza gave Heineken a big foothold in Mexico, one of the world's most profitable beer markets. Mexico sells most of its beer through what one might generously call convenience stores. While some of these 300,000 outlets are proper shops, most are 'mom and pop' affairs that are little more than private houses with a kiosk on the side where customers knock for service. This may sound primitive but, unlike Britain, the market is still growing.

By taking over Femsa, Heineken has improved the balance of earnings from mature and emerging markets – the latter now account for 40 percent. It has also maintained Heineken's position as a global force. It is ranked No 2 behind Anheuser-Busch InBev by profitability and is close to overtaking SABMiller as No 2 by volume. Heineken said that it expected the annual cost savings to be €150 million.

Questions

1. Explain as many reasons as you can why Heineken might have wanted to takeover Femsa Cerveza.

2. Explain why improving "the balance of earnings from mature and emerging markets" may be important to Heineken.

3. Assess the likely role of mergers and takeovers in Heineken's international success.

4. Discuss the impact on Mexican consumers and local businesses of Heineken's takeover.

Why do global industries grow inorganically?

There are many reasons why mergers and takeovers take place and they are often interlinked. Procter and Gamble (P&G) bought Gillette in 2005, in a deal worth $57 billion, to become the world's biggest household goods maker, pushing Unilever into second place. This was done not just to grow, increase market share and make more profit. It also removed a major competitor and gave P&G access to Gillette's important and lucrative portfolio of brand names. Between them, they share 21 brands that each have annual sales of more than $1bn. Not only that, their grooming brands complement each other; P&G specialises in hair and skincare for women, while Gillette focuses on male grooming. The deal also yielded cost savings of between $14bn and $16bn from economies of scale and internal restructuring.

Increase in sales, revenues and profits

Market share can be expanded rapidly by inorganic growth in the form of mergers and takeovers; something that is particularly important in some of today's rapidly expanding global markets. For most global industries the driving force is the profit motive. Increased market share means more sales, greater revenue and hopefully more profit. This rewards shareholders and management, and enables further investment and growth to take place.

Economies of scale and synergy

One of the primary reasons is to reduce average costs by achieving economies of scale. Falling costs can lead to reduced prices and a competitive advantage, or higher profits. These can be re-invested for more growth. In competitive global markets this can be all important.

When two companies come together, there is often duplication of resources. They may no longer need two head offices or two distribution depots. By disposing of surplus resources savings can be made and efficiency increased. Unfortunately for some people this re-structuring or rationalisation means that they lose their jobs. The P&G takeover of Gillette saw 6,000 jobs cut from the new, larger business.

Synergy is an added something that can be gained when two businesses join together. It comes from the Greek 'synergia', which means joint work and cooperative action. The word is used quite often to mean that combining forces produces a better product or business. For example a merger of two oil companies, one with a superior distribution network and the other with more reserves, would have synergy and would be expected to result in higher earnings per share than previously. In 1999 Exxon took over Mobil, expecting synergy in exploration and drilling, and also in terms of sharing technical expertise. The same year, BP took over Burmah Castrol, partly to get the smaller company's drilling rights in areas where BP did not have a strong presence, and partly to get the global lubricant brand, Castrol. But synergy does not always emerge in practice.

> **Synergy** is the idea that after a merger or takeover, the performance of a combined enterprise will exceed that of its previously separate parts. Sometimes this is expressed as 2 + 2 = 5.

Entering new markets

For some global businesses a merger is a very convenient way of entering into a new market. This can be a difficult process, fraught with unforeseen problems. Taking over an existing business reduces uncertainty. Supply chains and distribution networks are already in place and consumers are familiar with existing brands. This can be particularly important where markets are expanding rapidly and there is little or no time to enter and grow by organic means. Mergers and takeovers enable businesses to keep pace with dynamic markets. It may also be the case that entering new markets is the only way to expand as the established domestic markets may be saturated or even in decline. Such was the case with Heineken in the case study above.

SSL International

SSL is better known for its two international brands, Durex and Scholl as well as locally owned brands, such as Syndol and Meltus in the UK and Sauber and Mister Baby in Southern Europe. In 2007 it set out to expand its share of the world condom market. It entered new markets by taking over existing condom businesses. In Russia and Eastern Europe, SSL took control of Beleggingsmaatschappij Lemore BV, which makes Contex, Russia's top-selling condom and in Switzerland they acquired the Crest brand. SSL also bought out Qingdao Double Butterfly Group, its Chinese joint venture partner and opened a new £13 million factory, capable of making one billion condoms annually. By 2010 they had doubled sales and seen a 33% rise in profits. Then they were, in turn, taken over by Reckitt Benckiser, a consumer products giant in a $3.9 billion takeover.

Balancing investments in countries

As a global company expands by mergers and takeovers it builds up a portfolio of businesses. These may be similar to the main business or completely different in both nature and location, i.e. diversified. This provides both balance and stability in a global company. Those of you who have followed unit 2b may know these as 'risk-bearing economies of scale'. Having operations in different economies means that a downturn in one country is not as serious as it might be; other areas may be doing well. For example, in 2010 Heineken bought FEMSA beers, which had a large share of the beer market in Mexico and Brazil. In this way Heineken hoped to benefit from growth in emerging markets, balancing out falling sales in western markets such as the UK.

Tata is the largest Indian multinational company with operations in more than 80 countries across six continents. Its activities include IT services, vehicles, engineering, steel, consumer products and chemicals. In 2012 it earned revenues of over $100bn, more than half of it abroad, while employing around 450,000 people. Tata has balanced its investments by first of all moving beyond its domestic market and then extending its product portfolio to include a diverse array of products and services. It is perhaps best known in the UK for its acquisition of British brands such as Tetley's Tea and Jaguar Land Rover.

This diversification has clearly benefited Heinemann, Tata and Honda (below). Risks are spread and uncertainty is reduced by mergers and takeovers.

Honda motorcycles

In the recent recession, the motorcycle industry in the developed economies suffered a great deal. Motorcycles are now seen as luxury products and are income elastic. In Europe in 2009 Honda's sales of 276,000 bikes were down by 12% on 2008. In Japan, Europe and the USA sales were down by over a quarter of a million. However its sales in India for just one month in December 2009 were 375,808 bikes, a staggering 74% increase on the same month in 2008. (Yamaha could only manage 13,000 Indian sales in that month.) Honda sold 7.5 million bikes in Asia during 2009, a million more than 2008. Even though the Asian bikes are more basic, smaller and cheaper, they more than made up for its falling sales in the developed economies.

Acquiring brands and market segments

Brands can be very important for global businesses; they already have an established image and loyal customers. In many cases when a business is taking over another one, the brand is worth more than the physical assets that go with it. Not only that, but a readymade market segment comes with it. For a business that does not operate in that particular segment this is a useful and rapid way of expanding market share and reaching more consumers.

L'Oréal

Since the 1980s L'Oréal has pursued a successful programme of expansion by acquiring brands that both increase and complement its existing product portfolio. The brand names are important and are kept on, despite now being owned by another company. L'Oréal, the world's largest cosmetics company has transformed itself from an exclusively French company, narrowly focused on white women, into a global business whose skin, hair and cosmetics products are tailored to consumers all over the world. For example, in 1998 and 2000 it acquired Softsheen and Carson. These companies provided beauty products for the African American ethnic market in the USA.

Since then L'Oréal has built on this and used these brands to penetrate other markets such as South Africa. To speed up their expansion in China, L'Oréal acquired Mininurse, a Chinese mass skin-care brand, in 2003. In 2004 they bought Shu Uemura, a Japanese cosmetics firm. In 2006 they took over The Body Shop and in 2009 Urban Decay (a US cosmetics business), both brands that have strong ethical stances and are focused on a younger market segment. These are just some of the businesses acquired by L'Oréal, which seems to have a gift for identifying major growth areas, looking at the leading players and then moving in.

Of course, L'Oréal's success is not just down to mergers and takeovers. They have a highly effective marketing department and promote their products heavily. Innovation is also a key factor. They invest over 3% of their turnover (that's more than double that of their competitors) in developing new products and improving existing ones. The L'Oréal group are now active in 130 countries, through 290 subsidiaries and around a hundred agents. The company is active in three main sectors: cosmetics, dermatology and pharmacy.

Keeping up with the competition

As markets expand and become more open and global, some businesses may get left behind or have difficulty in keeping pace with the leading companies. A merger may help to maintain or increase competitiveness. BA (British Airways) and Iberia, Spain's national carrier, announced plans to merge at the end of 2009. The merger would allow the company to compete more effectively with other European giants including Air France-KLM and Germany's Lufthansa. In fact, since the merger the companies have struggled. The economic downturn hit air travel in general and the deep economic crisis in the Spanish economy caused many problems for Iberia. IAG (International Airlines Group) which owns BA made an operating loss of €278 million in the first three months of 2013. Meanwhile Lufthansa is reported to be in talks with Turkish Airlines (THYAO) over a possible merger.

These kinds of mergers are not just to do with keeping up with the competition; they have also been brought about by the pressures of the recent recession and a downturn in the number of passengers.

How effective are mergers and acquisitions?

Mergers and takeovers have a poor track record of success. Although the idea might look good on paper, less than 50% are estimated to deliver the anticipated benefits. There are several main reasons for this. The most blamed cause is the human element: different organisations can be very difficult to join together. There can be clashes of corporate cultures and management styles, and the workforce may be suspicious of change. There is also the danger that businesses become too spread out and move away from their core strengths. Mergers and takeovers tend to follow the economic cycle and increase when the economy is booming, but when times are hard many fall apart. A glance in the business section of the press will often show large numbers of firms selling off parts of their business (divestment). For every success story such as Procter and Gamble or L'Oréal, there is a BA and Iberia.

Chapter 15

Global marketing

Coca-Cola and the 2010 World Cup

Coca-Cola is one of the world's iconic brands. The traditional bottle shape and red and white labelling are recognisable everywhere. As a sponsor of the 2010 football world cup held in South Africa it planned a marketing campaign around the event. This included a World Cup Trophy Tour by Coca-Cola, which took the Trophy to 86 countries, including every nation in Africa.

A global TV commercial featured Roger Milla, the legendary African footballer from Cameroon, famed for his iconic celebratory dance during the World Cup in Italy in 1990.

Up-and-coming Somalian hip-hop artist K'Naan recorded an uplifting African-inspired track, a remix of 'Wavin Flag', as the anthem of Coca-Cola's World Cup programme. The track was used as the music element throughout the entire campaign including the soundtrack on all TV commercials.

In addition 250 teenagers from around the world gathered at a special football camp hosted by Coca-Cola in Pretoria, South Africa during the World Cup tournament. The camp encouraged young people to continue to be active through sports and included training, skills demonstrations, celebrity coaches and a tournament.

Questions

1. To what extent do you think that Coca-Cola was 'Thinking global and acting local'?

2. Assess the benefits of this approach for Coca-Cola.

3. Suggest two other marketing strategies that Coca-Cola could use. Justify your answers.

Global marketing refers to the marketing strategies used by businesses when operating in global markets. The elements of the marketing mix may be the same or different according to which part of the global market a business is in.

There are two opposing views that a business can adopt when considering a global marketing strategy.

The domestic approach (Ethnocentric Model)

On the one hand there are firms that tend to transfer their existing domestic business model to international business. This means that they see foreign markets as identical to their domestic markets. If it works at home, it will work over there. There is no necessity to change the design of the product, nor any of the associated marketing activities. The whole of the marketing mix can be standardised allowing a company to reap the rewards of economies of scale as it expands production and it can minimise the amount of time and resources devoted to individual markets. This may help to reduce average costs and give the firm a competitive advantage, but they risk losing sales because their marketing mix is not oriented to individual markets.

Ethnocentric Model: an approach to marketing based on the tendency to look at the world primarily from the perspective of one's own culture. A business believes that what was a success story in its domestic market will also be so in the other countries in which it operates. Foreign operations are treated as secondary or subordinate to the domestic markets. Products and services are therefore sold without adaptation.

The international approach (Polycentric Model)

As we have already seen in Chapter 12, there can be significant social and cultural differences in doing business between countries. For many firms operating on a global basis this means that they will need to adapt some parts of their marketing mix to maximise sales in different markets. Some businesses take this approach to extremes and develop a unique marketing mix to take advantage of each market's differing characteristics. Each individual market is seen as distinctive and so products and marketing activities (distribution, promotion and price) are all individually customised. This usually results in sales increases on a local basis but sometimes at the expense of profit. Customisation inevitably results in increased costs as there is a limited application for the economies of scale mentioned above and each individual market needs individual attention to the promotional message.

> **Polycentric Model:** an approach that considers each host country to be unique. Each of its subsidiary businesses develop their own unique business and marketing strategies in order to suit these particular needs.

The mixed approach (Geocentric Model)

There must be a happy medium whereby businesses can enjoy some of the advantages of a standardised approach, taking advantage of economies of scale, but at the same time catering for the needs of individual markets to maximise sales.

More sophisticated multinationals are recognising this and reorganising their global marketing plans in a new way, which could be described as the modularisation of marketing. The idea is simple: what needs to be managed globally is organised one way, and what needs to be managed locally another. In consumer markets, this tends to mean that concepts or platforms e.g. the brand and global identity are managed globally, while smaller markets are a local responsibility and adapted accordingly.

> **Geocentric approach** sees the world as a potential market with both similarities and differences in domestic and foreign markets. An effort is made to develop integrated world market strategies to gain the best from both of these strands.

Think global, act local

So perhaps the solution lies somewhere in between the two extremes. Some form of global standardisation is necessary with some customisation for individual markets. This is often summed up by the expression 'Think global, act local'.

> **Think global, act local** has been applied to many fields of work but in the business sense it can be described as how to achieve globalisation and still remain locally accountable.

To an extent Coca-Cola did that with their World Cup campaign. They have a clear corporate and global brand identity that is the same the world over, yet their campaign had a strong regional and African emphasis aimed at maximising sales at that point and in that area at that time.

They have adopted a similar approach in India. One of Coca-Cola's advertisements featured Bollywood star Hrithik Roshan. A group of youngsters go out for a late night snack, only to find the eateries shut. They meet Hrithik on the way and go on a magical midnight tryst with the star. Coca-Cola adds the fizz. The advert is aimed at India's students and young professionals who are looking for a bit of excitement in the new globalised environment. Some call it **glocalisation**, a saleable mix of the global and the local. The term was first used by social scientist Manfred Lange in 1989 on the eve of the Global Change Exhibition in Moscow.

> **Glocalisation** combines the words 'globalisation' and 'localisation' to emphasise the idea that a global product or service is more likely to succeed if it is adapted to the specific requirements of local practices and cultural expectations.

KitKat is one of the world's best known brands with roughly $2.0 billion in sales revenue in 2012. In the USA it has added sugar and less milk. In Japan it comes in a bewildering array of flavours including maple syrup, melon, vanilla bean, grape, apple, banana, caramel, kiwifruit, azuki, green tea, yuzu and cherry blossom. A three-finger KitKat is produced for the Middle East to match a denomination of the local currency, making the product a convenient, one-coin purchase. In Malaysia, KitKat is produced in a special formula for warm climates. Peter Brabeck, Chairman of Nestlé, said "Each of these product variations is the result of thorough market research on local tastes. There is no global consumer for the food-and-beverage business."

McDonalds

By the end of 2012 McDonald's had over 34,000 restaurants worldwide in 119 different countries. Clearly, with this kind of distribution the demographic, variations are enormous, particularly with their push into the rapidly growing Indian, Chinese and Asian economies. McDonald's is in an ongoing process of adapting restaurants and menus to cater for the types of people who are most likely to be customers in each individual nation.

There are many diverse influences to be catered for. In India, for example, the cow is a sacred animal for many Hindus and so they developed the Maharajah Mac which uses chicken rather than beef. Similarly in Saudi Arabia no pork products are served as it is prohibited by Islamic law. All meat sold is halal. In Israel there are both kosher and non kosher branches. Differing tastes lead to a large variety of offerings so if you fancy a McSpaghetti – spaghetti noodles served in sweet tomato-based sauce, hot dogs and grated pasteurised cheese – go to the Philippines. In south Korea try the McBingsoo (a Patbingsu sweet dessert with shaved ice), in Singapore try fish McDippers or the McSpicy. In Malaysia a bestseller is Bubur Ayam McD which literally translates to 'chicken porridge'. In Japan you can eat your Teri Tama Burger or Ebi Filet-O with seaweed flavoured french fries.

Yet despite all of this regional variety we would have no trouble in recognising the familiar golden arches with the red and yellow colour schemes of McDonald's anywhere in the world. The strength and identity of the global brand gives them a real competitive advantage and sends a clear signal to consumers everywhere. Yet it takes great care to tailor its products to an individual market's tastes to maximise sales. Love them or loathe them, this really is a business which has taken to the 'Think global, act local' message.

Questions

1. What evidence can you find to support the idea that McDonald's have a geocentric approach to their marketing?

2. Can you think of any disadvantages of McDonald's marketing strategies?

3. "There is no global consumer for the food-and-beverage business." (Peter Brabeck). To what extent do you agree with this statement?

Whilst it may be relatively straightforward for a company like McDonald's to adapt its products and marketing strategy to suit a number of different markets, other companies may struggle. In an industry such as consumer electronics, characterised by high product development costs and rapidly changing technology, there is a real need for developing globally standardised products and services. By serving large markets, development costs can be quickly recovered. Japanese companies such as Sony and Matsushita have been successful in marketing standardised versions of their products. Many of Sony's consumer electronics products are standardised except for the parts that meet national electrical standards. Apple, with their iconic range of products, follows a similar strategy.

The marketing mix and sales incentives

What all of these companies are doing is using the marketing mix as you might expect, but adjusting it to a greater or lesser degree to fit the circumstances. We have seen how products can be changed to suit the local market as with McDonald's, or not, as is the case with Sony or Apple.

Price is a crucial part of successful marketing in a global context. For some markets price will need to be low to attract consumers. The level of economic development may not permit standard western pricing tactics. The fast food companies moving into India know this and always have some low price items on their menus. The Nokia phone carries a low price. Levi Strauss has developed a lightweight pair of jeans for use in the monsoon season in India. They are expensive at 9,000 rupees but they dry out fast and Levi's have developed a 'pay-as-you-wear' scheme, so that buyers can pay in instalments.

Promotion is also tailored to suit local tastes and interests. Coca-Cola, as shown above, is a good example here, with its links to Bollywood and the World Cup. The Future Group in India is a chain of supermarkets that uses traditional ways of selling its products. Not for them the ordered and neat rows of products. Their displays are deliberately disorganised and live up to the idea of 'organised chaos'. This is because many Indian consumers are distrustful of neat, tidy displays because they suggest high prices. So their promotional displays are intended to mimic the traditional chaotic bazaars and kiranas (corner shops).

Place and promotion are neatly combined by Unilever's Shakti Programme, which helps women in rural India set up small businesses as direct-to-consumer retailers. The scheme equips women with business skills and a way out of poverty, as well as creating a crucial new distribution channel for Unilever products. This means that their products now reach millions of potential new customers in rural areas who would previously not have been able to access them. In 2012, 48,000 entrepreneurs, called 'Shakti Ammas', were selling products to over 3.3 million households in over 135,000 Indian villages. It is planned to expand this number to 75,000 by 2015. Similar schemes are now being introduced in Bangladesh, Sri Lanka and Vietnam.

Reverse innovation

Emerging markets such as the BRIC countries are rapidly becoming the new mass markets of the world. The customer base in these markets is very different in two crucial ways from those in developed markets. They are much less well off in terms of per capita income and there are many, many more of them.

Business analyst Vijay Govindarajan argues that glocalization means that MNCs target only the top of the pyramid in these markets, the wealthiest 10%. But the real potential lies in unlocking the other 90%. He says that adapting global products created for the US customers in a market like India simply will not work to capture the full opportunities in India. Future growth of multinationals may well depend on catering for this neglected sector of the global market. Reverse innovation holds the key.

Some MNCs are now using this idea (sometimes called frugal innovation). Rather than making products that become more and more sophisticated, they are looking very carefully at the needs of poorer consumers and designing new products with those needs in mind. This does not mean that costs are slashed and that the products are 'cheap and nasty'; far from it, they have to be tough and they have to work. Nokia now makes phones with a built in torch to cope with power cuts, several phone books for people who share a phone and menus in different languages. The Nano car is another example. Products like these are not just limited to the poorer economies; some analysts predict that the results of reverse innovation will spread back to the developed world. General Electric in India has developed a hand-held electrocardiogram which is less than half the cost of conventional ones and will ultimately find its way onto western markets.

Chapter 12 introduced some of the examples referred to above. In fact there are many aspects of social and cultural differences that play a key role in successful global marketing. This highlights the importance of analysing business and economic problems with reference to a wide range of ideas drawn from different topics. In any context, there are many links to be made when planning imaginative solutions to business problems.

Chapter 16

Exploiting global niches

A case study – Triumph Motorcycles

Despite falling bike sales in general and rising material costs, Triumph managed record sales in the UK in 2009 and overtook Kawasaki to become the fourth biggest seller. It has also become the world's fastest growing motorcycle brand and increased its global market share from 3.2% to 4.1% despite the decline in the global economy and the fall in worldwide sales due to the recession.

One of the factors in this success story is that Triumph is a niche brand with a reputation for high quality engineering, drawing on a carefully managed global supply chain. All the research, design and detailed engineering are done in the UK. Engines and suspension systems come from Japan, commodity components from China, and top-quality bolts and washers from Germany. The bikes are assembled in the UK via a highly developed flow production system.

The global market for larger motorcycles (+500cc) has fallen dramatically from 1,250,000 units in 2008 to just 690,000 in 2012. Despite this 45 per cent fall in global sales, Triumph has managed to more than double its global market share from 2.3 to 5.7 per cent. Over the same period, Triumph has doubled its design engineering capacity in the UK and grown its model range from 13 to 23 bikes.

Overseas expansion has played an important role in Triumph's success. The company has launched in 13 new markets including Argentina, Brazil, Columbia, the Czech Republic, Hungary, Russia and Slovakia.

Questions

1. How do you account for Triumph's success?

2. Assess the business risks that might face Triumph in the future.

Niche markets, subcultures and shared values and perceptions

For many customers faced with a delay in the arrival of their orders, there will be a temptation to reject that product and choose a substitute instead. The motorcyclists waiting patiently for their delayed Triumphs are however, happy to wait. For them the fact that it is a Triumph and not just a motorcycle is all important. Many of Triumph's customers will never have been to Britain but whether they are American, French or Japanese, they all share the same perception of Triumph as an iconic British brand. Motorcyclists themselves are a **subculture** with shared values; within that subculture there are further divisions that span continents. This idea applies to many different products from diverse fields such as fashion, culture and leisure. Many manufacturers know this and exploit these global market niches to gain a competitive advantage.

> **Subcultures** are groups of people who have interests and values in common. They may be based on hobbies, life-styles, ethnic or religious background or just personal enthusiasms and preferences. People who belong to subcultures do not necessarily communicate with each other but the internet makes it easy for some.

Gatorade makes a beverage that contains electrolytes and minerals used before, after, and during physical activity. It is aimed at athletes. A marketing analyst examined brand perceptions about Gatorade. The results showed that the subgroup of consumers who regarded themselves as real 'athletes' had a much stronger perception of the brand value and therefore loyalty to it, than 'non-athletes'. This enabled Gatorade to target the 'athletes' much more precisely and effectively with other products related to Gatorade.

Global market niches

Niche markets are covered in both unit 1 and in units 2a and 2b. A market niche is a smaller, more specialised segment of a larger market. For example, cars and clothing are both large markets, while hand-built sports cars and maternity wear are both niche markets within those markets. In niche marketing a company focuses on a particular niche instead of an entire market.

There are many benefits to niche marketing; by focusing on a smaller segment of the market, a business has the ability to provide specialised services and products which are often more valuable and in greater demand. Consumer demand can be more price inelastic which may enable a higher price to be charged. Direct competition may be reduced. Smaller markets also allow you to get to know your customers better and, as a result, develop effective marketing and sales strategies. This means the company is more able to satisfy the customer, which, in turn, leads to customer loyalty and repeat sales.

> **Global market niches** are smaller, more specialised parts of a global market where customers in more than one country have particular needs that are not fully met by the global mass market. The product or service is likely to be differentiated from that of the mass market.

A global market niche has very similar characteristics to local niche markets but operates on a global scale. Some global niches are large and some are very specialist and small. For some producers, production on a global scale is the only option as there is not enough demand in the domestic market to sustain the business. For others it is a way to escape the increasingly hostile competition from low cost foreign producers. By concentrating on a section of the market that has particular preferences and adapting their product accordingly, they can differentiate and escape direct competition.

There is a connection here to the idea of the 'Long Tail' where many scattered 'one-off' or 'niche' sales more than make up for a large number of 'mainstream' or 'hit' sales. The spread and increasing sophistication of the internet has helped the rise of the niche and global niche markets.

Philippines seek global coffee-market niche

The Philippines is taking tentative steps towards developing its status as a quality grower of the coffee bean. The Philippine Coffee Board knows that the country cannot compete with the likes of current regional exporting giants such as Indonesia and Vietnam, in terms of volume or price. So they are aiming for global niche markets and targeting the fast-growing number of young professionals who crowd cafes across the world.

The gourmet coffee products that the Philippines are starting to offer include special 'premium arabica' blends and the strong 'barako' bean that is favoured by Filipinos.

Special varieties found only in isolated areas are also being developed, as is production of 'Civet coffee' – made from beans eaten and excreted by Civet cats.

We have a lot of exotic coffees and that is the way to sell our products successfully," said Josefina Reyes, director of the board. In this way, they hope to be able to compete with the global giants. Their website offers many specialty coffees from the Philippines with delivery to anywhere in the world. They are expecting strong growth in exports of specialty coffee and hoping that the country can be a net exporter by 2017, with good customers amongst coffee shop chains like Starbucks.

1. Explain in your own words why the Philippines are aiming for a global niche rather than competing directly with countries such as Vietnam or Indonesia.

2. Why might they be targeting 'young professionals'?

3. How might the Philippine Coffee Board use the marketing mix to sell their coffees?

Global niche marketing is usually to do with marketing a differentiated or specialist product to one or more market segments. Many businesses operating in global niches are classed as small to medium size enterprises (SMEs). The EU defines these as businesses employing less than 250 staff. In fact some 99% of all businesses in Europe are classed in this manner, accounting for around 50% of all employment.

These global niches can be found in both mature and expanding markets. They do not include small firms selling undifferentiated products in a global market. Rather, they offer a product or service that is distinctive and clearly recognised as such by potential customers. Characteristics of successful global niche businesses will include:

- Clear understanding of the needs of their customers and their chosen market
- High levels of customer service
- Expertise in their field
- Prioritising profit rather than market share
- Innovation to satisfy change in the market
- Focus on cost efficiency but not at the expense of quality
- Using the marketing mix as appropriate for the differing market segments.

Wardell Armstrong

Wardell Armstrong Mining and Quarrying have been providing expert advice to the UK mining industry for over 170 years. In recent decades their mining services have expanded globally to cover specialised aspects of mineral resource exploration and extraction.

Projects include exploration and resource assessment of mineral reserves all over the world. They have offices in the UK, Kazakhstan and China. Recent projects have seen them at work in Kazakhstan, Mongolia, Russia, Peru and the Arctic.

Their specialised service means that they operate in a global market providing guidance and assistance to many different organisations, businesses and governments that lack the relative experience and in-depth skills.

The American University in Cairo Press

Established in 1960 the AUC Press has become the Middle East's leading English-language publishing house. Its goals and purposes reflect and support the mission of its parent university in education, research, and cultural exchange through professional publishing and bookselling services.

Its rapidly expanding publishing program of high quality scholarly, literary, and general interest publications on Egypt and the Middle East, currently offers up to 100 new books annually and maintains a backlist of some 800 titles for distribution worldwide. Through its bookstores and distributors in Egypt and abroad, the AUC Press sells more than 300,000 books every year and licenses foreign editions of Naguib Mahfouz (Nobel prize winner for literature) and other Arab writers in 40 languages.

Questions

1. What evidence can you find to suggest that Wardell Armstrong and the AUC Press operate in a global niche market?

2. What might the advantages be for them?

3. Are there any drawbacks?

Chapter 17

What are the benefits of multinational corporations?

A large multinational

Royal Dutch Shell plc, commonly known as Shell, is a global group of energy and petrochemicals companies of British and Dutch origin. Shell was listed as the world's second largest corporation by sales in 2013. The company's headquarters are in the Netherlands and its registered office is in London. Shell operates in more than 100 countries and territories and it employed more than 102,000 people worldwide. In 2012 it topped the Fortune Magazine's Global 500 list, the magazine's yearly ranking of the world's 500 largest corporations with a turnover of $484 billion

A small multinational

Innovia Films is a leading producer of speciality polypropylene and cellulose films for packaging and labels. The company's head office is in Wigton in Cumbria. Production is based on sites in America, Europe and Asia with sales offices throughout Europe and agents and distributors across the globe. With a turnover of over $595 million, the business employs some 1,400 people worldwide.

Questions

1. What advantages are there for businesses that have activities in a range of different countries?

2. How are host countries likely to be affected when foreign owned businesses locate there?

Multinational corporations (MNCs) are businesses that operate or have assets in more than one country. They are sometimes described as transnational corporations (TNCs) or multinational enterprises (MNEs). Such companies have offices or factories in different countries and usually have a centralised head office where they co-ordinate global management. The United Nations calculates that there are over 77,000 MNCs.

MNCs are nothing new. Early examples include the British East India Company in 1600, but they really began to develop early in the 20th century and proliferated after World War II. In recent years there has been a surge in the growth of MNCs. The spread of globalisation, the breaking down of trade barriers, the emergence of new markets, the liberalisation of existing ones and advances in information technology have all contributed to this.

They can be very large organisations with turnover exceeding the GDP of many countries. Inevitably this gives them great power and influence. Many MNCs have been accused of abusing their position and have attracted great criticism of their actions. But not all MNCs are large powerful corporations; many are small scale, like Innovia in the case study above.

- To their opponents, MNCs represent everything that is bad about global trade and globalisation. Their critics portray them as bullies, using their power to exploit workers and natural resources with scant regard for the economic or environmental well-being of any country or community.

- Their supporters see multinationals as a triumph for global capitalism, bringing employment, income and new technologies to poorer countries, driving up incomes and aiding development. In return, wealthier countries get cheaper goods.

Both viewpoints have some foundation in reality. The truth perhaps lies somewhere between the two.

In recent years there has been a surge in the growth of multinational companies.

Distrust of MNCs is nothing new. Writing in 1864, US President Abraham Lincoln wrote… "I see in the near future a crisis approaching that unnerves me and causes me to tremble for the safety of my country. …corporations have been enthroned and an era of corruption in high places will follow, and the money power of the country will endeavor to prolong its reign by working upon the prejudices of the people until all wealth is aggregated in a few hands and the Republic is destroyed."

Multinational corporations are businesses which are active in several different countries.

The biggest MNCs

Most of the largest MNCs are American, Japanese or European but countries such as India and China have large MNCs which are growing rapidly.

- Tata, the Indian conglomerate, has operations in over 80 countries across six continents and earns 58% of its income outside India.

- Sinopec, an oil, gas and petrochemical business and China's biggest company, is fifth in the top 10 of the Fortune 500 list of top corporations by turnover (2013).

- One third of all cigarettes produced are smoked in China. China National Tobacco, a state-owned enterprise, is the world's biggest cigarette producer and the only one in China. It plans to expand in South America and Eastern Europe.

Tables 17.1 and 17.2 show the data on MNC size. It is very likely that the biggest MNCs of the future will be Chinese or Indian and that they will come to dominate the global economy. If that seems doubtful, it is worth remembering that not so long ago the idea that a Finnish producer of rubber boots would go on to dominate the global market for mobile phones and that Nokia, in turn, would be overtaken by Samsung, a Korean chip maker, seemed equally unlikely.

Table 17.1: Top global companies, 2012

Rank	Company	Revenue $ millions	Profit $ millions
1	Royal Dutch Shell	484,489	30,918
2	Exxon Mobil	452,926	41,060
3	Wal-Mart Stores	446,950	15,699
4	BP	386,463	25,700
5	Sinopec Group	375,214	9,453
6	China National Petroleum	352,338	16,317
7	State Grid	259,142	5,678
8	Chevron	245,621	26,895
9	ConocoPhillips	237,272	12,436
10	Toyota	235,364	3,591

Source – Fortune magazine/CNN

Table 17.2: Turnover of the 5 largest MNCs by comparison with 5 countries' GDPs

Rank	Country/Company	GDP, Nominal estimated revenue ($ millions)
7	United Kingdom	2,445,408
24	Norway	485,803
1	Royal Dutch Shell	484,489
2	Exxon Mobil	452,926
3	Wal-Mart Stores	446,950
25	Argentina	446,044
27	South Africa	408,237
4	BP	386,463
5	Sinopec Group	375,214
28	United Arab Emirates	360,245

Source – Fortune magazine/CNN and World Bank

There is a tendency to see MNCs as expanding from the west into emerging markets. In fact the majority of investment by MNCs still takes place in developed economies. Examples in the UK include the car manufacturers Toyota, Honda and Nissan. Toyota, the world's biggest car manufacturer has also expanded significantly in the USA, arguably hastening the downfall of the US motor industry.

Why have they grown?

- **To access new markets:** for many MNCs, domestic markets are saturated. Future growth and rising profits must come from expansion overseas where rising incomes can be tempting. Entering new markets can form an extension strategy for the product life cycle. Products which are in maturity or even decline can take off again and continue to yield profit. For example, the tobacco companies that face declining domestic markets, PMI (Philip Morris International) and BAT (British American Tobacco) both have aggressive expansion plans in developing country markets. These have attracted much criticism from anti-smoking pressure groups. For example, in 2013, BAT is investing $200 million in new production facilities in the Philippines. (Chapter 1 looked at the lure of new markets in more detail).

- **To reduce costs:** expansion overseas can yield substantial cost savings. There may be economies of scale leading to lower unit costs and enhanced competitive advantage, especially if the product can be standardised for a range of markets. However, the most significant factor is the ability to take advantage of lower resource costs. Unskilled labour may be cheaper, more available and less regulated. Now, many countries can offer labour that is cheap, skilled and adaptable as well. The global management consulting firm A.T. Kearney's Global Services Location Index (GSLI), a ranking of the most attractive off-shoring destinations, noted this trend. The Baltic states are emerging as a key destination because of their well-educated labour force and a recent 35% fall in wage rates. For example Lithuania is 14th in the GSLI ranking and Barclays have opened an IT centre in Vilnius. Labour is not the only cost that can be saved; proximity to markets can also be significant. (Chapter 2 covered this in detail.)

- **To control resources:** many businesses have to follow the resources to extract and process them. Companies that rely on a secure and preferably cheap source of raw materials are likely to expand where they are found. Examples include minerals, petrochemicals and many commodity industries. MNCs are currently vying to gain access to Arctic and Antarctic mineral and oil reserves. Chile and Bolivia contain much of the world's lithium reserves (23% and 40% respectively). Lithium batteries are commonly used today to operate computers, cell phones, and other portable electronic devices. Demand may increase dramatically if electric cars are mass-produced and consume a growing share of the market. MNCs such as SQM (the world's largest lithium producer) and countries such as Korea and China are keen to gain access to these reserves but the Chilean and Bolivian governments want to make the most of this potentially valuable resource.

- **Taking advantage of governments and getting round trade barriers:** many governments offer substantial incentives to attract MNCs to their countries. In 2009 Dell computers moved its manufacturing plant from County Limerick in Ireland to Lodz in Poland. A major factor in this decision was a €52.7 million aid package offered by the Polish Government. Also in 2009 a measure introduced by eight Beijing municipal government departments offered any MNC which sets up its regional headquarters in Beijing a subsidy of up to RMB10m (just under £1m). Businesses that wish to penetrate markets and avoid tariffs or quotas will often move production into that area. Toyota began to produce in the USA to access NAFTA markets. (Chapter 13 looked into the reasons for this trend.)

- **Because they can:** advances in travel and technology have made it much easier to organise and co-ordinate business operations around the world. Email and video conferencing have made some travel obsolete. New trade blocs, market liberalization and the WTO, the expansion of India, opening up in China and the fall of communism in Europe have all encouraged the spread and growth of MNCs.

Benefits that multinationals bring to host countries

Multinationals are often welcomed in host countries as they can bring many benefits with them. These benefits apply to a range of stakeholders including the people, the government, other businesses and the economy as a whole.

Google

Google recently opened a second headquarters in the business district (Puerto Madera) of Buenos Aires, Argentina. The new office in Argentina will act as the regional hub for the company, managing not only Latin America but also providing some services to the Spanish market. Before Buenos Aires, Google had headquarters in the USA and Ireland. The company now employs about 2,000 workers with further expansion planned over the next few years. The Argentine government supports Google's operations in their country because jobs are created for its citizens.

NISSAN – North-East England

Trying to avoid tariffs and delivery charges in the EU, Nissan chose to build its car plant at Washington in North East England. This was partly due to government incentives but also the area had a rich industrial heritage and a strong reputation for engineering skills backed up by specialist colleges and universities. It had good roads and access to two deep water ports. The first car rolled off the production line in 1986.

(continued overleaf)

It wasn't just the workers directly employed who benefited. A major manufacturer draws other firms to the area to supply it with components. TRW, an American corporation, opened its first UK plant in 1988 at Peterlee, County Durham, to make seat belts. In 1989, TRW set up a second factory at Rainton Bridge, Sunderland, to make electrical switches for vehicles. In 1993, TRW opened a £25 million high precision engine valve plant in Washington, supplying Nissan, Ford, Rover and Vauxhall.

Since 1986, Nissan has invested over £2.5 billion in the area. It employs 5,000 people directly and another 15,000 are employed indirectly in the supply chain. These jobs may be threatened should the UK decide to leave the EU, particularly if Nissan decides to re-locate elsewhere.

Questions

1. Why would the UK government have been willing to offer incentives to Nissan?

2. Explain why other firms such as TRW may have moved in to the area.

3. Assess the factors that may have led to Nissan choosing the Washington site.

Employment

Starting operations in an overseas country involves a flow of capital into the economy to fund the creation of productive capacity (FDI). Even if help is offered by the host government there will still be considerable direct expenditure. Even a modest sized production plant will require land and materials for construction. Often these materials and the labour needed will come from the host country. Builders, joiners, electricians and others will be needed to complete the project. All of this will create local employment and income.

Once the plant opens it may employ many local people – depending upon the skills needed and the skills available. Often managers from the parent country will run the operation and employ and train local people. Once production starts the plant will create more employment for other businesses. Supplies and services will be needed and this is an opportunity for local firms to start up or expand existing operations. An MNC may need raw materials, components, transport, maintenance services, cleaners, packaging materials and so on. This creates employment and income, some of which will be spent in local shops and businesses, increasing demand for other goods and services, creating more employment. In other words a positive regional multiplier effect occurs. Indirect job creation is estimated, by the UN, to be 3 to 7 times the jobs directly generated by MNCs respectively in the manufacturing and food industries.

PepsiCo – Ireland

PepsiCo Ireland first came to Cork in 1974, producing concentrate base for well established brands such as Pepsi, Diet Pepsi, 7Up, Mountain Dew, Sierra Mist, Mirinda and Gatorade at a plant at Little Island. In 2003 PepsiCo invested over $100m in a state-of-the-art second manufacturing facility at a greenfield site in Carrigaline. In 2006 a satellite R&D centre was also established at Little Island.

In 2007 PepsiCo transferred its Worldwide Concentrate headquarters from New York to Cork, where it oversees PepsiCo's entire global concentrate operations. A new pilot R&D plant was also established. In 2012 PepsiCo added a new R&D centre for next-generation products, costing €10m.

PepsiCo Ireland now employs over 600 people at its three locations in Cork. The business activities located in Cork include the manufacture of concentrate (exported to 105 countries worldwide), laboratories, financial shared services (supporting 65 countries), IT providing support to global operations, R&D and Global Market Intelligence.

Questions

1. Suggest reasons why PepsiCo chose Cork as a location.

2. Analyse the impact PepsiCo may have had on Ireland's economy.

3. Assess the impact PepsiCo may have had on local people and local businesses.

Effect on wages

One source of confusion, not to mention controversy, is wages. MNCs are often accused of paying 'low wages', yet this can be misleading. Low in comparison to what? We may not be willing to work for wages at that level but that does not mean that those workers are being underpaid or exploited. Wages must be looked at in the context of that country.

There is a common belief that MNCs are exploiting workers by paying very low wages and keeping employees in sweatshop conditions. Yet academic research and studies do not support this. Jagdish Bhagwati, economist and author of *In Defence of Globalisation*, argues that a raft of empirical studies has been conducted in Bangladesh, Mexico, Shanghai, Indonesia, Vietnam and elsewhere, and the findings are straightforward. Far from exploiting the rock-bottom wage rates generally paid in the poorest countries, multinationals tend to pay well above the going rate in the areas in which they are located. In the case of US multinationals, pay is often 40 percent to 100 percent above local wages.

There are reasons for this. Higher wages will provide a larger pool of labour from which to choose. This increases the chances of finding workers of the right calibre. Workforce turnover should be reduced, which cuts costs. Well-paid workers may be more motivated and more productive than low-paid ones.

Paul Glewwe, a leading development economist looked at Vietnam and found that the average wage-earner received US23c an hour, but workers in foreign-owned businesses made an average of US42c an hour. When Glewwe conducted his work, 15 percent of Vietnamese were classified as very poor and 37 percent as poor. But nobody working for multinationals was classified as very poor and only about 8 percent were poor. He also found that women seemed to benefit disproportionately from MNCs. "Two-thirds of workers in foreign-owned businesses in Vietnam are women, and nearly two-thirds are in their 20s, confirming that globalisation is driving social change and female emancipation."

Of course, this is not to say that all MNCs are wonderful, benevolent organisations dedicated to their worker's welfare. As we shall see later some MNCs have appalling track records.

Skills and technology transfer

FDI from an MNC brings with it a set of skills and technology, of which the host country may have little or no experience. Although the skills and technology are used by the MNC for its own benefit, some of them will 'rub-off' or transfer to the host country. The degree to which this happens depends on the nature of the business and the complexity of the process.

When a new business opens, some of the jobs it offers may require training which the MNC can provide. As the local workers are trained they become more skilled and this increasing skill level can benefit the local and national economy. MNCs often teach local workers the skills necessary to operate sophisticated production systems. The training MNCs offer is transferred when employees change jobs. Locals trained as managers gain insights into business activities that might otherwise not be available to them. By developing closer links with domestic suppliers, MNCs, through their subsidiaries, can transfer valuable techniques to domestic businesses.

Technology, like knowledge and skills, transfers to local economies through supply linkages, competition, and labour turnover. Systems otherwise unavailable to local economies become available when they are imported by MNCs. Experience of machinery and know-how, including production and engineering techniques, may not be available to local enterprises and their presence can be a catalyst for innovation among local entrepreneurs.

Many MNCs have found, to their dismay, that industrial espionage and copycat production can be a hazard when locating abroad. Copyright and IPR can be difficult to protect, China has long been notorious in this respect, although things have improved significantly over recent years. Subcontracting arrangements introduce new technologies to local businesses, giving them the opportunity to enhance or adapt new techniques for the domestic market.

The benefit to the host country of technology transfer is particularly important for its export industries. Advanced equipment reduces production costs; combined with relatively inexpensive labour, it may lead to

lower prices and increased volume, making the host country more competitive. Export promotion is an important part of many countries' growth strategies. The Chinese appliance maker Haier (see below) has undoubtedly benefited from flows of FDI which have changed work practices and standards there. Along with many other firms it is now exporting its goods to the developed countries. Much of the growth in the economies of Taiwan, Hong Kong and South Korea is due to technology transfer including technical know-how, managerial skills and marketing techniques.

Haier

In the 1920s a refrigerator factory was built in Quingdao to supply the Chinese market. After the1949 communist Revolution, Haier was taken over and turned into a state owned enterprise (SOE).

By the 1980s the factory had debts of over ¥1.4 million and suffered from dilapidated infrastructure, poor management, and lack of quality controls, resulting from the centrally planned system. Production had slowed down to such an extent that production rarely passed 80 refrigerators a month; the factory was close to bankruptcy. Salvation came in the form of a new young manager Zhang Ruimin who was appointed as managing director in 1984.

Zhang decided to use Western and Japanese business practices and management techniques. When he arrived in 1984, he realised that the poor condition of the factory's quality controls was endangering its continued survival. Zhang achieved the transformation through a joint venture with a German appliance maker, Liebherr. They transferred the technology and know-how to manufacture household appliances.

The factory began its recovery by licensing refrigerator technology from Liebherr. The installation of Liebherr's equipment and technology was accompanied by a new and rigorous commitment to quality. Haier adopted its name from the 'herr' in the German company's name.

"The first year, we had 600 employees and 300,000 yuan ($35,000) in sales. We were bankrupt," Zhang said. Since then, Haier has expanded to 18 factories in China, making 9,000 products that range from microwave ovens to a machine sold in South Korea for drying herbal medicine. In 2008, it launched its own lines of cell phones and laptop computers. In 2012, Euromonitor International ranked Haier as the number one major appliance brand in the world with 8.6% retail volume share and sales of over $25.8 billion. Haier has 61 trading companies, 24 manufacturing plants, and 21 industrial parks with 80,000 employees worldwide and has developed into a giant multinational company.

Question

Assess the significance of technology transfer in the transformation of the business.

Effect on the wider economy

MNCs should have a wider beneficial impact on the economy of the host nation whether it is a sophisticated developed economy such as the UK or a developing economy such as Vietnam. Increases in employment and wage levels should generate a larger taxpayer base, providing the government with increased revenue. At the same time there may be a reduction in government expenditure if some form of benefits had previously been paid to the unemployed. The multiplier effect will increase this as well. Profits from MNCs can be taxed, again adding to revenues which can be used to further development.

Export revenues can be generated and provide funds that can be used to buy much-needed imports. Mining accounts for about 5% of Tanzania's GDP and a third of exports. In 2011 the value of mineral exports reached $2.1 billion; more than 95% of that came from six gold mines. The Tanzanian government received about 10% of those revenues. Production from MNCs can help to replace imports and improve the trade balance.

CSR and the positive impact on communities

Many multinationals have CSR and ethical policies that they try to adhere to. To the extent that they succeed, they will often prove to be the kind of employers that many people really want to work for. If MNCs take care to offer better pay than local employers, they will usually be looked on favourably. However, many businesses are seeking low-cost labour and freedom from onerous regulation. They always say that they obey the laws of the host country but this does not necessarily mean that they take employee welfare seriously.

Some companies go beyond simply improving on local wage rates. They try to help the local economy to develop. (See Chapter 11 for more detail and case studies.) Others want to help by devising products that will address the greatest needs of poorer people in the communities where they operate. Bernard Giraud, Director of Sustainable Development and Social Responsibility at Groupe Danone, said "Selling to the poor is not sustainable business. It is not simply about affordability… the products and services provided must bring clear social value to the impoverished."

Grameen Danone Foods ltd.

A joint venture was started by Danone and the Grameen Bank (the 'Bank of the poor') in March 2006. They launched a yoghurt called Shoktidoi, designed to meet the nutritional needs of Bangladeshi children and improve their health. It is made from local cow's milk and date molasses and sells for just 5p.

The whole of the production and distribution system has been constructed with the aim of creating as many jobs as possible within the local community. Local farmers provide the raw materials and also benefit from micro-credits offered by the Grameen Bank to start up or expand their businesses. Danone provides technical expertise. The pots are entirely biodegradable. Shoktidoi is distributed using a system based on the so-called 'Grameen Ladies' who make sales door-to-door. They receive a small commission on each pot sold.

By 2009 sales stood at 32,477 pots per day, but the pilot plant was still operating below capacity. Plans to expand had to be shelved. The yoghurt was in fact selling much better in the cities than in the countryside. But production continues and future expansion looks likely.

Question

In what different ways can CSR contribute to alleviating poverty in the least developed economies?

Conclusion

The advantages that MNC investment brings to host countries can be considerable. MNC involvement and FDI can be a major driver of growth and a route out of poverty. China is a good example of this; FDI in 2012 was $119.7 billion as the country's recovery from the global economic downturn attracted more overseas money.

It is not just the poorer nations that have much to gain. We should not forget that the majority of FDI still finds its way to the richer economies. Despite the economic recession, the United States is still the world's largest recipient of FDI. In 2008 more than $325.3 billion in FDI flowed into the United States although this had dropped to $234 billion in 2012.

Nevertheless there can be significant drawbacks to MNCs as we shall see in the next chapter. For many people, the harm that MNCs can do outweighs potential benefits.

Chapter 18

The costs of multinationals

Indian Retail

AT Kearney's Global Retail Development Index has identified India as the most attractive destination for retail business. It will become one of the top five retail markets of the world in 10 years time. Retail is the second-largest sector in India's economy after agriculture and accounts for 7 percent of employment and 10 percent of the country's GDP. It is estimated to be worth over $330 billion and is expected to grow by 25% over the next few years. This growth is being driven by a rapidly expanding middle class, and rising GDP and incomes.

Naturally the big MNCs such as Wal-Mart and Tesco are keen to gain a share of this lucrative market. However the Indian government has a policy of allowing 100% FDI in cash and carry wholesale markets but only 51% FDI in single brand retailing. This limits the pace of expansion by foreign MNCs. 97% of Indian retail trade consists of small shopkeepers.

When the government announced that it would relax its rules and allow more foreign MNCs to operate in India, Wal-mart announced expansion plans with their joint venture partner Bharti. Thousands of small shopkeepers mounted protests in the major cities. Traders in Delhi burnt images of Bharti and Wal-Mart executives during protests against the move. In Mumbai protestors threatened to boycott the sale of Sim cards and top-up vouchers that power the Bharti mobile network. As a result the government abandoned its plans to allow foreign MNCs to operate as single brand retailers.

In 2012 the Indian government finally gave approval to the long-delayed plans to open up the retail sector to more foreign investment. All was well for foreign MNCs until early 2013 when the government, facing more protests and a forthcoming election, reversed its decision and once more restricted access to the Indian retail market for foreign MNCs.

Questions

1. Why might the Indian Government be keen to limit the expansion of foreign MNCs?
2. Can you see any drawbacks to this?
3. Assess the impact of MNC expansion on (a) India's consumers and (b) India's small shopkeepers.

Even a cursory glance at the internet reveals many sites detailing the wrongdoings of MNCs. Some sites specifically monitor individual companies, such as Tescopoly (Tesco), Chevwrong (Chevron), McCruelty (McDonald's). At the time of writing there were over 160 different anti-Microsoft sites!

Just as you should be wary of what you might find on these companies' own websites, you also need to be careful of sites criticising MNCs. Both are trying to push their own agendas. This is a political minefield; many people see MNCs as villains in the light of anti-globalisation or anti-capitalist stances. The case study above shows the scope for controversy.

What are the potential negative impacts of multinationals on host countries?

Critics argue that far from MNCs creating wealth and employment wherever they go, the opposite is true. A range of charges are made against MNCs:

- MNCs are driven by an obligation to their owners and shareholders to make a profit. Little if any benefit spills over into the local economy, especially if **transfer pricing** is used to reduce tax obligations.
- Local businesses suffer at the hands of the MNCs who take away their market share. They mass-produce standardised products, threatening national product variety.
- MNCs may not train local workers to a high level. Skills may be brought in with expat workers and the

locals just used for unskilled labour. R&D facilities may be kept in the home country with little opportunity for technology or skills transfer.

- Many MNCs enter another country simply to access a new market, so only sales and marketing offices are established. There are few, if any, benefits.
- MNCs are likely to flit from one country to the next taking whatever incentives are on offer, before moving on to the next and newest low cost location, leaving behind unemployed workers and a weakened economy.
- When they do use local labour, wages and conditions are unsatisfactory leading to accusations of exploitation and sometimes sweat-shops and child labour.
- MNCs cause great damage to the environment by their processes and the transportation of their products. This damage can be short or long term and is usually unsustainable.
- They act as an agent for cultural imperialism which replaces and even destroys the native culture with unwanted products and values.
- They encourage a so-called '**race to the bottom**'.

> **Race to the bottom** – a phrase used to describe the way MNCs move to the country that offers the lowest tax rates or the weakest environmental controls. In order to hold onto their MNCs each country will offer them successively more advantageous terms at the expense of their own economy or environment, until the potential benefits of having an MNC are outweighed by the costs.

Transfer pricing

One of the claimed benefits of MNCs is that they will increase a host country's tax revenues. MNCs should in theory pay tax on profits earned in that country. One way round this is transfer pricing. MNCs buy and sell within their organisation between different national offices because each is a separate profit centre. For example, a company makes a product in Ireland for sale in continental Europe. To do this, it sells to its sales office in Paris. The Irish office charges a much higher price (transfer price) to its French Office than it might otherwise do, meaning, that on paper, the French office shows little or no profit and the Irish office makes a very large profit. This makes sense: the rate of corporation tax (tax on profits) at the time of writing is only 12.5% in Ireland but 33.33% in France. This has the effect of reducing the tax paid by the MNC and increasing its profits at the expense of, in this case, the French Government.

> **Transfer pricing** occurs when one part of an MNC in one country transfers (sells) goods or services to another part in another country. The price charged is the 'transfer price'. This may be unrelated to costs incurred and can be set at a level which reduces or cancels out the total tax paid by the MNC.

Each country has a different tax system, with detailed rules as to how tax is paid. With the use of some clever tax accountants MNCs can 'minimise', if not avoid, their tax liabilities. News Corps and Rupert Murdoch have long been controversial in this area. At a time when companies such as Walt Disney, Time Warner and Viacom averaged a tax rate from 27.2 percent to 32.5 percent, News Corp averaged 5.7 percent.

In 2013 many large companies faced public outrage when they were accused of tax avoidance. They included Starbucks, Google, Amazon and Apple. Almost two-thirds of Apple's $34bn (£22.5bn) global profits for 2011 were earned by companies registered in Ireland. Apple paid an average of less than 1% tax to the Irish government, leading US politicians and tax professors to accuse the group of deliberately moving around its global profits in order to lower its tax bill.

Negative impact on local businesses

Sometimes multinationals may have a negative impact on local firms. If they receive favourable treatment from the host governments, such as tax breaks or other forms of financial assistance, they are effectively

being subsidised. Local firms may become less competitive, lose market share and see a fall in profitability. It is often the case that the newer and usually more efficient MNC operations require less labour than the local businesses that close.

- This happened in Nigeria when Shell (Anglo-Dutch), Chevron (US) and Texaco (US) started operating there. Local firms, such as the Nigerian National Petroleum Corporation (NNPC) lost their prominent market position.

- In 2009 Wal-Mart opened a wholesale store in India, Tesco already had a joint venture there with Tata and Carrefour runs a fully-owned cash-and-carry business, with four wholesale outlets. Despite the re-introduction of restricted access regulations in India for large foreign retailers, there is still widespread concern amongst India's countless small retailers that many of them will lose their livelihoods.

- Toyota's move to manufacture in the USA hastened the demise of the US motor industry. Fifty years ago, American car companies dominated the world, especially General Motors, many of whose factories were based in Flint, 40 miles north of Detroit. Today there are only 6,000 GM workers in Flint, compared to 100,000 at its peak, and the town and workers are suffering.

Exploiting the workforce

Charges leveled at MNCs refer to sweatshops, child labour, anti trade union practices, poor health and safety records and the general exploitation of labour. Many household names such as Nike, Gap and Primark have been accused of such things. It is perhaps important at this stage to distinguish between MNCs that outsource by setting up their own production plants and those that buy from local suppliers. It is much easier to control working conditions with the former than with the latter, where complex supply chains can sometimes hide very real problems. An accusation that can be leveled at some MNCs is that they are sometimes not as strict or as careful about their source of supplies as they could be.

Current examples include MNC seed companies such as Monsanto, Syngenta, Unilever and Bayer. They have been accused of exploiting child labour on Indian cotton farms, where they work long hours and are exposed to pesticides. According to UNICEF, globally nearly one in six children aged 5-14 are engaged in child labour. The ILO (International Labour Organisation) estimates that throughout the world, around 215 million children under 18 work, many full-time. Whilst the majority of MNCs have nothing to do with the direct exploitation of child labour, this is often not the case for some of their suppliers.

In Malawi, one of the poorest nations, it is estimated that more than 75% of the population are directly or indirectly employed by the tobacco industry, which accounts for two thirds of its foreign exchange earnings. Malawi has an estimated 1.4 million child labourers, one of the highest incidences of child labour in Africa. Many of them work on tobacco farms for their families who are tenants and produce the crop for their landlord who sells it on to the big tobacco companies. Many of the children suffer from high levels of nicotine poisoning. The unregulated use of pesticides has led to further accusations of malpractice on many tobacco estates. The International Tobacco Growers Association opposes the use of child labour. Nevertheless, some of the world's biggest MNCs, including BAT (British American Tobacco) buy their tobacco from these sources. They use their monopsony power to drive down prices, depressing wages and perpetuating the need for children to help the family out by working rather than going to school. BAT claim that they are acting responsibly and have co founded the Eliminating Child Labour in Tobacco Growing Foundation (ECLT). Critics say that this is just a small scale PR exercise.

MNCs are sometimes charged with failing to ensure that proper health and safety standards are applied. In less developed economies laws and regulations may not be as stringent, or as rigorously applied. This may encourage some MNCs to cut corners and save money. In some cases the consequences for the workforce and host country can be very serious indeed. Since 2005, there have been several years in which over 1,000 workers in Bangladesh died in fires or building collapses. By far the worst incident happened in 2013, when 1,129 workers were killed after the collapse of a factory building at Rana Plaza in Dhaka. Primark, Bonmarche and Matalan were among a number of high street chains supplied by the factory. The retailers strongly deny a direct causal link and since then have joined other brands including H&M and Marks & Spencer in a legally binding building safety agreement. They have each agreed to contribute up to $500,000 (£325,000) a year towards rigorous independent factory inspections and the installation of fire safety measures.

Elsewhere Wal-Mart, despite some recent environmental changes for the better, remains anti-union and continues to offer low pay and limited benefits. It strongly opposes living wage initiatives. Nearly half the children of its US employees have no health insurance or have to get coverage from taxpayer-funded programmes. Phillips-Van-Huesen, owner of brands such as Tommy Hilfiger, Timberland and Ted Baker, has been criticised for closing a factory in Guatemala because the workers tried to form a union to protect their basic rights.

Environmental impact

In the BP Oil Spill in the Gulf of Mexico in 2010, more than 200 million gallons of crude oil was pumped into the Gulf of Mexico for a total of 87 days, making it the biggest oil spill in US history. A total of 16,000 total miles of coastline were affected, including the coasts of Texas, Louisiana, Mississippi, Alabama, and Florida. It had a devastating effect on the environment and wildlife. For many people this is symptomatic of the careless way in which big business has a negative impact on the environment.

Grasberg mine is owned by Freeport, the world's lowest-cost copper producer. It has the largest gold mine and the third largest copper mine in the world, located in the heart of Mount Jaya in West Papua. It is home to three of the world's eight remaining equatorial glaciers. It is a sacred site for the indigenous people inhabiting the region and depending on its ecosystem to survive. The mining process has destroyed huge sections of the mountain top leaving a massive open pit visible from space. The mine uses more than a billion gallons of water a month and has been accused of dumping 230,000 tonnes of toxic waste into the Ajkwa rivers each day, killing all plant life along its banks and contaminating drinking water supplies. Both Freeport and its partner Rio Tinto have been excluded from the investment portfolio of The Government Pension Fund of Norway, the world's second-largest pension fund, due to criticism over the environmental damages caused by the Grasberg mine.

It is difficult to assess the true cost of environmental damage caused by business activity, (this is explored in unit 4b). According to a recent study for the UN, published in 2013, primary production and processing in such sectors as agriculture, forestry, fisheries, mining, oil and gas exploration and utilities cost the world economy $7.3 trillion a year in damage to the environment, health and other vital benefits for humankind. The majority of the costs are from greenhouse gas emissions at 38 per cent, followed by water use (25 per cent), land use (24 per cent); air pollution (7 per cent), land and water pollution (5 per cent) and waste (1 per cent).

A case study – MNCs and Orang Utans

Oil companies have been accused of causing destruction to rainforests and wildlife by secretly adding palm oil to diesel that is sold to millions of UK motorists. Twelve oil companies supplied a total of 123 million litres of palm oil to filling stations in 2009. Only 15 percent of the palm oil came from sustainable resources. The rest came from land previously occupied by rainforest.

Large areas of rainforest are destroyed each year by companies seeking to take advantage of the world's growing demand for biofuels, which produce fewer emissions than fossil fuels because crops absorb carbon dioxide as they grow. It is not just the oil companies at fault here; many food products that you buy at your local supermarket also use palm oil as an ingredient.

The problem is that clearing rainforest to create biofuel plantations releases vast quantities of carbon stored in trees and soil. It takes up to 840 years for a palm oil plantation to soak up the carbon emitted when rainforest is burnt to plant the crop. Some three-quarters of these new plantations are alleged to have been planted illegally.

Indonesia has the greatest rate of deforestation, losing an area the size of Wales every year. The orang-utan has been pushed to the brink of extinction in some areas. Indonesia is now the third-largest CO_2 emitter, after China and the US.

Cultural imperialism

> **Cultural imperialism** is the practice of promoting, distinguishing, separating, or artificially injecting the culture of one society into another. It is usually the case that the former belongs to a larger, economically or militarily more powerful nation and the latter belongs to a smaller, less important one.

MNCs are often blamed for their role in the erosion of local and traditional ways of life. Their products swamp and replace products from the local culture. It is not just the products themselves; critics argue that this also brings in mainly western ideas and, in particular, American ones. The imposition of this alien corporate culture is seen as a retrograde step.

With over 33,000 branches in 123 countries McDonalds serves 68 million customers a day. The golden arches are now, according to Eric Schlosser's *Fast Food Nation*, "more widely recognised than the Christian cross." At a primary school in Beijing, it was found that all of the children recognised the image of Ronald McDonald, saying that "…he understood children's hearts." McDonald's may be an easy target but the same idea applies to drinks such as Coke, fashion, music, entertainment and lifestyle. It is not just the developing economies that are vulnerable to this; France saw a huge outcry when McDonald's first opened its restaurants in Paris.

Footloose MNCs

There is no guarantee that an MNC once located in another country will stay there. International markets are dynamic and volatile and an MNC may decide to pack up and move on. This can leave the host economy with various economic problems, the most obvious perhaps being a rise in unemployment, both directly and indirectly via the negative regional multiplier effect. Rising unemployment means lost tax revenue and possible increased expenditure on benefits if they exist. The host government will lose out on future tax revenues and export earnings. In short the loss of an MNC means a reversal of many of the benefits associated with the arrival of an MNC in the first place.

Loss of a major employer can also cause other MNCs to follow suit. Ireland has seen Dell shift some of its operations to Poland and there are fears that other high tech firms such as IBM may do the same. It is estimated that the loss to the Irish economy of Dell is worth some 5% of its GDP.

There are many reasons why an MNC may change location. Government inducements can be important, as with Dell in Ireland and Nissan in the UK. It can be a need to become more competitive and reduce costs, often by moving to a lower wage economy. Cheaper labour may not be the only attraction. More skilled and better educated workers may be needed.

Moving on…

Swedish manufacturer and supplier of outdoor power products, Husqvarna, eliminated 200 jobs in Tandsbyn, Huskvarna, Höör and Ödeshög. The restructuring was expected to streamline operations and increase efficiency. As part of the restructuring plan, the factories in Huskvarna and Höör were moved to Poland while the factories in Ödeshög and Tandsbyn were closed.

Pharmaceutical company Teva announced 315 redundancies at its Waterford plant, which manufactures inhalers and tablets. Tablet production was transferred to a plant in Hungary. There were 730 workers employed at the Waterford site.

The Danish based multinational medical company, Coloplast, announced in 2009 that it would close the factory in Espergærde (north of Copenhagen) and 400 workers would be made redundant. Production moved to Hungary.

Questions

1. Suggest two reasons why these businesses moved their production plants.
2. Why might moving its factories to Poland increase efficiency for Husqvarna?
3. Assess the effects of Waterford's move on (a) its workers and (b) the Irish and Hungarian economies.
4. What might the Danish government have done to persuade Coloplast not to move production? Assess your suggestions.

Saints or Sinners? – a conclusion

Imagine a world without MNCs; no Apple, Shell, Sony, Ford, McDonald's, Bosch, Yamaha, H&M and so on. It is difficult to see life as we know it without these familiar brand names. Without MNCs we would have to rely on our own resources; choice would be limited, prices would be higher and innovation would be well below the level we take for granted. Very few people would like to see the back of MNCs.

The trickier question is, to what extent are they a positive or negative influence on their host country? You have already read some of the views and case studies supporting each side of the argument. Many people have a very negative view of MNCs, not helped by numerous examples where MNCs have acted appallingly, both in the past and in the present: Nike with its past use of child labour, Primark and Matalan's alleged links with unsafe factories and poor working conditions, the current environmental damage of the palm oil industry and the actions of petrochemical companies. It is perhaps inevitable, although certainly not excusable, that such incidents occur.

The enormous size and economic strength of some MNCs compared to the national income of their host countries does little to dispel this image. There is evidence that some MNCs have paid bribes to government officials in order to get around obstacles erected against profitable operations of their enterprises. In 2012 the multinational pharmaceutical company Pfizer paid a US$60.2 million fine to settle a US government probe of the drugmaker's use of illegal payments to win business overseas. But these negative influences must be seen in the context of both the sheer number of MNCs and the disproportionate adverse publicity that they attract. Many MNCs have done much to improve their actions whether pushed by public opinion, legislation or just plain altruism. For example Nike now features in the top 20 out of 581 MNCs in the Covalence Ethical Rankings table. By contrast however, Chevron is languishing in the bottom 5 places.

If we put aside these negative influences and any political prejudices and begin to examine the situation more closely, a different picture begins to emerge. Just as Adam Smith described with his 'invisible hand' idea, the drive for profit and reward leads to the creation of wealth for others. Evidence supplied by the World Bank and United Nations strongly suggests that MNCs are a key factor in the large improvement in welfare and reduction in poverty that has occurred in developing countries over the last forty years. By contrast countries that have seen little involvement with MNCs, such as those in sub-Saharan Africa, have developed more slowly.

A report by Robert Stern and others at the University of Michigan concluded that "However, as an empirical matter, …there is virtually no careful and systematic evidence demonstrating that, as a generality, multinational firms adversely affect their workers, provide incentives to worsen working conditions, pay lower wages than in alternative employment, or repress worker rights. In fact, there is a very large body of empirical evidence indicating that the opposite is the case." Other studies support this conclusion; the idea that MNCs all exploit labour and treat their workers badly does not bear scrutiny. This does not mean that such practices do not happen. They do; the supply chain for many large MNCs is very complex and it is not always possible to monitor every small supplier effectively.

It is of course not just the developing countries that have benefited from the development of MNCs. We in the developed world have also seen our living standards rise. We have access to a wide and varied range of necessities and luxuries. So, Saints or Sinners? It will probably not surprise you to learn that MNCs are neither. Much depends upon your social and political viewpoint but they are neither evil capitalist tools of oppression nor paragons of virtue.

Chapter 19

Can multinationals be controlled?

Plan A

In 2007 Marks & Spencer announced a 100-point five-year plan to re-engineer itself. Stuart Rose, the Chief Executive, said "It's called 'Plan A' because there is no 'Plan B' for either M&S or the planet." M&S claims that it is responding to public opinion and that 97% of its 15 million customers are telling it that it must behave responsibly. The company said that there were 'compelling commercial – as well as moral reasons' to introduce the plan.

The aim of Plan A is that M&S will:
- become carbon neutral
- send no waste to landfill
- extend sustainable sourcing
- help improve the lives of people in their supply chain
- help customers and employees live a healthier life-style

Plan A had 180 commitments and by 2013 M&S claimed to have met 139 of these targets and claimed a benefit of £185 million so far.

Questions

1. What do you think the company meant by saying that there were 'compelling commercial – as well as moral reasons' to introduce the plan?

2. To what extent do you think that there is a tradeoff between becoming more sustainable and profitability?

3. Assess the benefits to M&S of Plan A.

By their very nature MNCs are hard to control because they transcend national boundaries. There is no such thing as a 'world government' or 'world court' that can prevent MNCs from doing what they want or force them to modify their behaviour. As we shall see some efforts have been made by the UN and other bodies to exert some influence over MNCs but with varied success. Such control as there is comes from a number of factors.

- Public opinion
- Pressure groups
- The media
- Self regulation
- Government control & regulation
- Legal regulation.

In practice it is often a combination of these factors that comes in to operation. Public opinion can lead to the creation of **pressure groups** which may mount media campaigns to persuade the MNC to modify its actions or persuade Governments to intervene or bring about legal proceedings.

Public opinion, pressure groups and the media

In many ways these three factors are inseparable. Public opinion may well lead to the creation of pressure groups or pressure groups may help to form public opinion. Pressure groups often rely on the media to publicise their actions, which in turn can further influence public opinion and so on.

Public opinion has done much over recent years to influence the behaviour of many MNCs. This is particularly true for those companies that rely on consumer loyalty and their brand name. Retail firms like M&S provide good examples of this. Or think of Nike: after much damaging publicity over sweatshops and the use of child labour in some of its suppliers' factories in the 1990s, sales dropped as the public showed their disapproval. Similar allegations were made about Gap and both businesses were quick to change their supply chain policies to placate customers. More recently Primark has faced similar problems following reports made by the TV programme Panorama and the linkage to the factory that collapsed in Bangladesh.

> **Pressure groups** are organisations that express the opinions of people with common interests. They attempt to influence governments and corporate policies regarding their particular concerns and priorities.

One area in which pressure groups are particularly active is the environment. Some large companies that have failed to practise good environmental management have been targeted by campaigners. Pressure groups often represent large bodies of consumers and widespread opinion, so it can be important for a company to maintain good relations with them. Greenpeace is perhaps the best known environmental pressure group in the UK.

In 1995, Greenpeace found out about plans to sink the obsolete 14,500 tonne Brent Spar oil storage platform owned by Shell, in deep water. Activists then occupied the Brent Spar to stop this happening; the action was part of a campaign to stop ocean dumping. Greenpeace came into conflict with both the UK government and Shell. The media took up the story using dramatic shots of activists being attacked with water cannons and relief teams being flown in by helicopter. This did much to stir up public opinion against Shell.

The public responded by boycotting Shell garages across Europe with up to a 50% loss in sales in some areas. Despite the UK government's refusal to back down on plans to allow the Spar to be dumped into the ocean, public pressure proved too much for Shell, and the company agreed to dismantle and recycle the platform on land. The decision led to a ban on the ocean disposal of such platforms by the international body which regulates ocean dumping.

Greenpeace, Palm Oil & Unilever

Greenpeace is currently running a campaign to highlight the environmental impact of the global increase in demand for palm oil. They have campaigned against companies such as Unilever, which produces many of Britain's best-known household brands such as Flora and Stork margarines, Dove toiletries and Persil. It is also the world's biggest consumer of palm oil. Their report *Burning Up Borneo*, released in 2008, linked deforestation to Unilever's suppliers through the use of maps, satellite data, and on-the-ground investigations.

On 1 May 2008, Unilever Group Chief Executive Patrick Cescau announced that all Unilever's palm oil will be certified sustainable by 2015. He also said that Unilever was supporting the call for an immediate moratorium on any further deforestation in Indonesia for palm oil plantations. In 2009 and 2010 Unilever terminated two contracts with suppliers that were thought to be involved in the destruction of rain forest. In 2013 it announced that it had reached its target of 100 per cent certified sustainable palm oil three years ahead of its original schedule. The World Wildlife Foundation (WWF) says that 31 of the 132 companies it surveyed received a top score for their use of sustainable palm oil. The Indonesian Minister for Agriculture, Gatot Irianto, has called for environmental groups to "stop demonising palm oil".

Questions

1. Why might Unilever have decided to use only sustainable palm oil?

2. Why might the Indonesian Minister not support Greenpeace's campaign?

3. Assess the impact of Unilever's decisions on (a) its shareholders and (b) palm oil suppliers.

The Internet

The Internet is becoming more and more important in monitoring and controlling MNCs. In the previous chapter we mentioned some of the sites, such as Tescopoly and Chevwrong, that critically report the activities of particular companies. These are very useful ways of disseminating information and rallying support and undoubtedly have some influence. More recently the internet has been used in other ways such as Twitter, YouTube and Facebook to publicise issues. It is now possible to motivate individuals in a way that was impossible before the creation of the internet.

At the end of March 2010, Nestlé bowed to pressure to make the palm oil used in the manufacture of its products such as KitKat, Aero and Quality Street more eco-friendly. This followed a guerrilla campaign waged against it on the internet. The centrepiece of this campaign was a spoof advert against KitKat, mimicking its 'Have a Break' advert. It showed an office worker biting into a KitKat containing an orangutan finger, which dripped blood onto a computer keyboard. This was a reference to the damage done by the unsustainable use of palm oil to orangutans, a close relative of man which lives only on the heavily deforested islands of Borneo and Sumatra. Over 1 million people watched the advert on YouTube and many of them posted angry messages on Nestlé's Facebook page – substituting the word Killer for KitKat. Greenpeace also disrupted Nestlé's annual general meeting. Protesting 'orangutans' greeted shareholders and, inside the building, activists unfurled banners with the message: "Nestlé, give the orangutans a break".

Self regulation

A growing number of companies are taking the steps to control and modify their own behaviour either by adopting and strengthening their own policies of CSR or joining an umbrella organisation such as the UK government backed ETI (Ethical Trading Initiative) and EITI (Extractive Industries Transparency Initiative), or the Fairtrade Foundation, and adopting their ethical codes.

CSR by itself is of little importance in regulating the behaviour of an MNC. A quick glance at the websites of the bottom 5 companies in the latest Covalence Ethical Rankings table will show that they all have a comprehensive CSR policy in place! Yet clearly some MNCs, whether for reasons of commercial pressure or altruism, are attempting to change the way they operate. Marks & Spencer as shown above is a case in point.

The Ethical Trading Initiative (ETI) is an alliance of companies, trade unions and voluntary organisations. All members of ETI agree to adopt the ETI code of labour practice which is based on the standards of the International Labour Organisation (ILO). Their aim is to improve the lives of workers across the globe that make or grow consumer goods – everything from tea to T-shirts, from flowers to footballs. The purpose of EITI is to make companies and governments publicly disclose how much they earn and the amount they pay to the developing countries where they operate.

The Fairtrade Foundation is the independent non-profit organisation that licenses the use of the FAIRTRADE Mark on products in the UK in accordance with internationally agreed Fairtrade standards. The businesses that join initiatives like these must adhere to the standards set down by the organisation. The tradeoff is likely to be an enhanced brand image in the eyes of consumers and potentially increased sales.

One drawback of ethical codes is that they may focus the MNC's attention on addressing only one issue and ignoring other problem areas.

Legal enforcement & regulatory structure

All countries have a legal framework under which businesses must operate. One way of controlling the behaviour of an MNC is to seek legal redress by taking the company to court. Unfortunately this can be difficult because MNCs are not under the control of any one legal system. It can be difficult to hold a parent company liable for the actions of one of its subsidiary companies. However, in 2012 BP received the biggest criminal fine in US history as part of a $4.5bn (£2.8bn) settlement related to the fatal 2010 Deepwater Horizon disaster. BP also set aside another $3.85bn on top of the $38.1bn it has set aside to cover its liabilities. The UK-based oil giant has sold some assets to raise the funds.

In some countries the legal system can be difficult to use and success is uncertain. When attempting to tackle large and wealthy MNCs the legal proceedings can be lengthy and costly. Again, Chevron is facing an ongoing legal battle over its alleged pollution of the Ecuadorian rainforest, displacement of indigenous peoples and a legacy of cancers and birth defects caused by the contamination. The proceedings have been going on since 1993.

Facebook, Twitter and YouTube have been used to publicise issues concerning MNCs

Sometimes though, legal proceedings are effective. In 2010 German carmaker Daimler pleaded guilty to corruption charges in the US and paid $185m (£121m) to settle the case. The charges related to investigations into the company's global sales practices. Daimler, the owner of Mercedes-Benz, admitted to paying tens of millions of dollars of bribes to foreign government officials in at least 22 countries. The company said it had now reformed the way it did business. In 2010 Toyota was fined $16.4m (£10.7m) for failing to inform the US government of safety concerns surrounding faulty accelerator pedals.

In 2010 The US Environmental Protection Agency imposed a $2.5 million penalty on Monsanto to resolve misbranding violations relating to the sale and distribution of cotton seed products containing genetically engineered pesticides. In 2013 a Brazilian court fined Monsanto $250,000 for misleading advertising concerning GM soya beans.

Regulatory authorities such as the Competition Commission in the UK, and the EU equivalent in Brussels, can sometimes control aspects of MNC behaviour. They have far reaching powers and the ability to levy fines of up to 10% of a firm's turnover if they act against the public interest. Coca-Cola was found to have used its power to stifle competition by insisting its customers in shops and bars stocked only their products in their fridges. Now, when Coke supplies a free-branded fridge to retailers with no other means of cooling drinks, 20% of its shelf space must be given over to products from other companies. In 2008 The European Commission imposed fines, totalling €1.3 billion, on Asahi, Pilkington, Saint-Gobain and Soliver for illegal market sharing, and exchange of commercially sensitive information regarding deliveries of car glass in Europe. The Commission is currently investigating the activities of MNCs in a number of industries as diverse as televisions, bananas and electronic components. Even countries in such dire straits as Zimbabwe are able to use the regulatory authorities to good effect. The Zimbabwean subsidiary of BAT (British American Tobacco) had to change its policies after they were found to have been using predatory behaviour against new entrants into the market.

Government control

Much will depend on the relative power of the MNC and host country. Probably the strongest country in relation to MNCs and so most able to regulate their actions is China. Its huge market with a potential 1.3 billion customers acts as a powerful incentive for businesses to accept the limitations and controls of the strong regulatory Chinese state. Even though the restrictions on foreign businesses in China relaxed slightly after they joined the WTO, all forms of business require state approval before starting. Whether it is a joint venture, a representative office or a wholly owned foreign enterprise, the relevant paperwork, license and approval must be gained. These of course, can be revoked by the state at any time.

All governments can control business activity to a certain extent and there are many ways of doing this. It may take the form of a licensing agreement as in the case of India and China or the government can insist on a joint venture before allowing access to the market. Restrictions can be placed on the degree of foreign ownership: requirements can be made to use a certain percentage of local labour; controls can be placed on the number of foreign personnel allowed into the country and so on.

In Australia the government has attempted to gain more of the lucrative revenues from the mining industry

by levying a supertax on MNC profits. In retaliation Fortescue Metals threatened to withdraw $15 billion of investment projects in the country. At the time of writing this is still unresolved.

In reality much depends on the relative power of the state and the MNC. A country hungry for FDI may be less fussy than say, China, where everyone wants to invest.

Chinese AMEA (Anti-Monopoly Enforcement Authorities)

China is the world's largest importer of iron ore and in April 2010 China announced that it had started an anti-monopoly review on a proposed iron ore joint venture between mining giants BHP Billiton and Rio Tinto, amid growing fears over pricing. China's anti-monopoly legislation requires firms to get Chinese government approval before their merger if their aggregate global revenue exceeds 10 billion Yuan (US$1.5 billion) or if revenue in China exceeds two billion Yuan.

For violations against monopoly agreements and abuse of a dominant position, the AMEA has the power to fine companies between one and 10 percent of total annual turnover plus the confiscation of any illegal gains.

Regulators in Australia and Europe are also reviewing the tie-up between the mining companies, which account for more than one-third of the total global supply of iron ore, on fears that their joint venture threatens the market. Steelmakers have appealed to regulators to "tackle competition distortion and excessive pricing" after iron ore miners attempted to increase prices by "80 percent or more".

Questions

1. Why might the Chinese regulatory authorities want to investigate the activities of BHP Billiton and Rio Tinto?

2. What factors might determine their success in controlling the Iron ore companies?

3. To what extent do you think they might be successful?

Conclusion: Can MNCs be controlled?

The extent to which it is possible to control MNCs depends upon the circumstances and the relative power each agent holds. For example the Chinese government is much more likely to be able to control or modify MNC behaviour than the Zambian government. The legal and regulatory framework in the EU is much tougher and more comprehensive than in many developing nations. A company such as Shell is much more able to withstand pressure to change than a much smaller MNC. Issues such as damage to the environment are much more likely to arouse public opinion than transfer pricing or tax avoidance.

MNCs are now much more likely to amend their behaviour than previously. A combination of globalisation, modern communications and technology mean that their activities are now much easier to observe and scrutinise. Public opinion is much more swiftly engaged and mobilised and many businesses are now more sensitive to that pressure. More and more MNCs are claiming to act responsibly, either as a selling point, or from genuine altruism. Governments are able to use both legislation and direct control to modify the actions of MNCs.

However, not all governments are willing to control aspects of MNC behaviour; some are simply corrupt or inefficient or lack the will to try. For some governments there can be a trade-off between appeasing public opinion and the need for the economic stimulus that MNCs can bring. Inevitably, some MNCs continue to behave in a way that is less than desirable. Pollution and negative externalities still happen and pressure groups are still as active as ever.

It would appear that as with so many complex issues there is no clear cut answer to the question "Can multinationals be controlled?"

Chapter 20

Where are we now?

During the late 1990s and early 2000s, the global economy was growing fast and economies appeared to be responding in healthy ways. This period has come to be known as 'The Great Stability'. But hidden behind the scenes, the growth in borrowing and lending that underpinned the growth of trade had gone too far. Confidence and enthusiasm had bred carelessness and greed.

The flow chart records the sequence of events that led first to the 'Credit Crunch' and then to 'The Great Recession'. It shows how the financial markets reacted to overspending. But beneath the financial froth the real economies of many countries had nose-dived. Their big problem was loss of competitiveness.

- Greece, Ireland, Portugal, Spain and to some extent Italy had lost competitiveness. They were members of the eurozone, so their currency could not depreciate to make them more competitive again. Germany, meanwhile, was becoming ever more competitive, partly because it is really good at manu-facturing technologically advanced products and partly because the euro could not appreciate to reduce Germany's advantage. The value of the euro was determined by the eurozone's average competitiveness, so it was too high for the suffering southern members and too low for Germany. Germany acquired a large trade surplus while the southern eurozone countries acquired large trade deficits.

- China was steadily increasing its exports and getting more technologically competent. The USA (and many other countries) were importing more and more from China, which acquired a massive surplus of dollars and other currencies. For some time, the Chinese government kept its exchange rate down by lending these surplus funds to its customer countries (especially the USA).

- By 2008, these trade deficits were worryingly large (in the UK as well as the USA and distressed eurozone countries). This added to the loss of confidence in the financial markets.

- As the recession developed, unemployment rose, tax revenue fell, unemployment benefit payments rose and public sector deficits grew rapidly.

Increased mortgage lending in many countries, 2000-2006

↓

Growth slows, downturn in housing markets, 2007

↓

Banks accumulate bad debts, as house prices fall, 2007-08

↓

Confidence in banking system collapses, 2008

↓

Banks drastically reduce all lending activity, 2008-09, the 'credit crunch'

↓

Reduced liquidity leads to widespread and lasting recessions, 2009 onwards

↓

Public sector deficits rise as GDP falls and unemployment rises, 2009 onwards

↓

Heavily indebted governments have to pay higher interest rates, 2010

↓

Some governments close to default, especially where there is external deficit, 2010 onwards

Most governments concluded that they needed to reduce borrowing: the deficits had got far too large. Two clever economists called Reinhart and Rogoff published research which said that if the accumulated deficit got above 90% of GDP, economic growth would decline. So governments started to cut spending, some faster than others. Some had no choice because the financial markets were refusing to lend them any more money, except at very high interest rates. These cuts reduced the demand for goods and services all over the world and businesses in the developed countries found their sales revenue falling. Of course they reacted by cutting their labour forces or cutting pay (or both). Most ordinary people found that one way or another, they were worse off. The public sector deficits got larger as tax revenue fell further and the cost of unemployment benefit rose. (These are the automatic stabilisers.)

That is where we are at the time of writing (2013). Various knotty problems are in the news:

- Youth unemployment has risen dramatically, over 50% in Spain, for example.

- 'Austerity' policies have reduced incomes in Greece by 25% and falling. The Greek people are seriously upset about this and riots have become commonplace.

- The German people object to bailing out governments that have large deficits. No one knows how this will affect the eurozone, although Mario Draghi, the head of the European Central Bank says that the ECB will do 'whatever it takes' to preserve the euro and the euro itself is not unpopular. Negotiations continue.

- In the UK there is a long-standing debate about Plan A (more austerity) and Plan B (get the economy moving and then cut the deficit later). Plan B is based on keeping incomes from falling any further. Revised data showed that UK GDP fell 7.2% from its peak in 2007 to the trough in 2009. By early 2013, it was still 3.9% below the peak.

Signs of hope

There is no doubt that the expansionary monetary policies adopted in many economies have prevented a major depression like that of the 1930s. Central banks kept interest rates phenomenally low from 2008 onwards and lent money to banks in the hope that businesses would be able to borrow funds for investment, so creating jobs. In the UK, quantitative easing (QE) pumped liquidity into the banking system in an attempt to replace the funds lost in the credit crunch. Similar policies were adopted in the USA and the eurozone.

- In the USA, there are signs of a return to economic growth, despite government spending cuts. Just possibly, the UK economy may be beginning to improve.

- Some countries have managed to increase their exports to China, India and other emerging economies where growth has slowed only slightly, so far. Spain and the UK are on the move with this.

- Extensive discussions have led to some measures to reform banking systems, making them safer.

- Some governments that have worn out or inadequate infrastructure are talking about investing public money in improvements that will create jobs.

- There is talk of structural reforms that could make uncompetitive economies less so. 'Structural reform' usually includes reducing employment protection, increasing competition between rival businesses (e.g. by stopping price fixing) and improving training in scarce skills.

- Shale gas is coming. In a few years the USA will be self-sufficient in energy. Possibly energy prices will fall world-wide.

> **Watch out** – for news on future progress. Work out who are the likely gainers and who are the losers from each change. For example, which of the structural reforms mentioned above will be likely to appeal to businesses, and why?

Potential anxieties

When aggregate demand is low, most businesses are having trouble selling their products. They won't invest unless they can see scope to expand their markets. **Austerity** is not good for businesses that rely on rising incomes. If it is causing an **increase in the public sector deficit**, it may be counter-productive. Mr Osborne's promise to end expenditure cuts by 2015 looks impossible.

Early in 2013, the theory that if the public sector deficit is above 90% of GDP, growth will falter, came under fire. Other economists questioned the quality of Reinhart and Rogoff's data. They also took the view that many countries' public sector deficits were caused by the financial crisis of 2008 and the subsequent bailouts and recession, rather than by earlier heavy spending. Mr Osborne resolutely stuck to Plan A, even though the deficit was still slowly increasing, despite his big expenditure cuts. The very slow economic growth kept tax revenue down and welfare spending up.

> **Follow the news** – try to separate the political knockabout from the facts.

The **loose monetary policy** that has helped to keep the recession under control will at some point pour too much money into the economy and encourage an acceleration in inflation. The Bank of England has to time the **exit from quantitative easing** at just the right moment. It must not stop while the economy is still growing painfully slowly but it must not go on for so long that it creates excess demand that pushes up prices. Judging the right moment to stop QE won't be easy

> **Mark Carney**, the new Governor of the Bank of England, will have much to say about this. Follow the story.

The UK is especially vulnerable because even during the recession it has had **skill shortages**. These were addressed by recruiting abroad but current immigration policy is making this difficult. It would be a good idea to train more people in scarce skills but this is not as easy as it sounds.

> **Think about your career** – are you considering going into the financial sector? If you are, you are probably equally capable of becoming an excellent engineer and could personally address one of the worst skill shortages.

Other issues

While the politicians have been preoccupied with the financial crisis, which throws up new problems nearly every day, there have been other developments in the world economy.

- **Inequality** has increased globally and not everyone is happy about it. The news about businesses (and individuals) who indulge in **tax avoidance** has raised many ethical issues.

- The **ageing population** has significant implications for economies.

- There are potential **resource constraints** that could affect many economies. **China**'s response is to expand its interests in **Africa**.

- **Climate change** carries on regardless, but many politicians have given it little thought lately.

- Dissatisfaction with the **European Union** could lead to a reformed and more effective organisation, or to total chaos.

Inequality and tax avoidance

In the UK, bankers' bonuses infuriated most people. They seemed to go up regardless of the performance of the bank and were given to employees who had quite clearly managed their banks' affairs incompetently in the run-up to the credit crunch. But in fact, globalisation created numerous opportunities for entrepreneurs and people with scarce skills to make money everywhere.

In theory, in countries where there are political parties that favour redistribution of income through the tax and welfare systems, inequality can be much reduced. But in practice this often does not work, because:

- Tax avoidance (reducing tax liability by clever accounting, so as to exploit loopholes in the system) is legal and much used especially by MNCs.

- Tax evasion (concealing income from the tax authorities) is widespread all over the world.

- Some countries have low tax rates, numerous loopholes and limited welfare benefits – as in China.

Will the oil run out? Like many resources, as it gets scarcer the price goes up making it profitable for companies to source it in more inaccessible places.

In democracies, voters can change the way they vote but even this may not make a big difference if the politicians listen carefully to business and other vested interests. There is a risk of political instability if public frustrations end in riots and disorder, which can threaten even a healthy economy. Careful choices have to be made.

Without tax avoidance and evasion...

...it is possible that the public sector deficits that gave so much trouble, 2009 onwards, would have been small and easily manageable. In 2012-13, Starbucks, Amazon, Apple, Google and others all came under fire for organising their international affairs with a view to minimising tax.

- They said: "we always operate legally. If politicians don't like the result they should change the law." But of course, they pay the best accountants to look for the craftiest ways of avoiding tax, and can do that again if the law changes.

- The UK Treasury said: "we are considering following the Swedish model, whereby you can be prosecuted for *aggressive tax avoidance*." This may happen but it will all turn on the legal definition of '*aggressive*'.

The ageing population

Growing numbers of elderly and relatively low birth rates mean that the number of working age people supporting the dependent population is falling in most places. (Only in Africa and some Asian countries are there still large numbers of young people and change is coming there too, though more slowly.) Politicians have been very slow to address this. Even in Europe some people are still opposing the raising of retirement age, even though they have few ideas about how to finance future pensions. This issue needs far more attention than it is getting.

Resource constraints and the environment

My students used to tell me the oil would run out. They didn't understand that as it got scarcer, the price went up, creating an incentive to look for it in more inaccessible places. Although oil and many other resources are indeed finite, not much is going to run out any time soon. Also, when specific mineral products get scarce, smart businesses do more research and find alternative ways forward.

What does happen is that prices rise. We have already seen this with oil and food prices. Chinese people are getting richer, buying more cars and eating more meat (and the same is happening in other fast growing economies too). China is securing raw materials by developing mining operations in Africa. Food manufacturers like Unilever are buying more palm oil, which encourages investors to burn rain forests in Indonesia in order to create new oil palm plantations.

While the politicians were grappling with the financial crisis and the subsequent recession, they put the environment on the back burner. It is time for more careful thinking. Luckily the pollution in Beijing's streets is now so bad that the Chinese government knows it has to do something, even though it has so far refused to be tied down by international agreements. When pollution gets really bad the question of whether climate change is man-made or not seems rather irrelevant. This one is not going to go away. It might be better if the oil did run out.

The European Union

The recurring crises in the eurozone have destabilised the EU. Those problems of competitiveness, covered on page 111, were going to happen anyway, but combined with the financial crisis from 2008 onwards, the problems grew bigger. For the eurozone, there are plenty of proposals, though none of them can secure easy agreement:

- A banking union – a common set of rules for all the banks in the eurozone, including common systems for the protection for depositors.

- An agreed role for the European Central Bank (ECB) as it tries to ensure monetary stability.

- A commitment on the part of Germany and other member countries to rescue struggling member countries that are unable to pay their debts.

- A rescue fund sufficiently large to recapitalise banks that fail.

At the present time, German voters do not like having to rescue the banks or the governments of other countries. But if the eurozone is to endure, they may have to. Imagine the Federal government of the USA refusing to rescue California if it were facing the collapse of its economy due to lack of competitiveness.

With the eurozone in such difficulty it is quite difficult for the 28 members of the EU to contemplate reforming the EU in ways that would make it work better. This means that the people who want a referendum in the UK, on whether to stay in or leave the EU, are asking us to decide on the basis of how the EU is now, rather than how it might be in the future. Mr Cameron may think he can negotiate a new deal soon but if the eurozone stays in deep difficulty, those negotiations may be impossibly difficult.

A referendum could be the beginnings of real trouble:

- The EU was originally formed as a way of keeping Europe at peace. As such it has been astonishingly successful.

- The US government does not want a UK exit and is not likely to be sympathetic.

- UK businesses that rely on exporting to the EU will suffer very badly indeed from an exit. If their sales fall they will make many people redundant.

- Nissan and other businesses that have brought much FDI to the UK, so that they could manufacture within the EU, may depart.

Think – very carefully. You might have your own list of the advantages of an exit for yourselves – but compare them with the above.

Index

Absolute advantage 57
Advertising 54, 69
Allocative efficiency 25
Anti-competitive practices 25, 109
Anti-dumping duties 73
ASEAN 27
Asian Tigers 16, 18, 44, 76
Austerity 111-13

Barriers to trade 2, 53, 95
Beggar-thy-neighbour policies 2, 18, 74
Brazil 41-42
BRICs 17, 29, 40-44

Capital movements 20
Centrally planned economies 42
Child labour 102
China 28-34
Climate change 33
Commodity prices 33, 41
Common Agricultural Policy 24, 60
Common external tariff (CET) 24
Common markets 19, 22
Communication costs 13-15,
Communism 28, 32
Comparative advantage 57-58
Competition 3, 7, 25, 27, 74
Competition policy 7, 33, 109-10
Competitive advantage 59, 82, 85, 95
Competitiveness 17, 26-7, 59, 84, 111
Consumer profiles 46-7
Containerisation 3, 14-15
Convergence criteria 27, 115
Corporate cultures 65, 68, 84
Corporate social responsibility (CSR) 61-2, 99
Corruption 105, 109
Costs of growth 21
Credit Crunch 3, 111
Cultural differences – see social and cultural differences
Customer loyalty 90

Declining industries 2, 75
Depreciation 26
Devaluation 18
Developing economies 16-17
Developed economies 16-17
Differentiated products 91
Diversification 83
Division of labour 56-7
Doha Round 76
Dumping 73, 77

Economic cycle 84
Economic growth 17, 24-5, 29, 40, 73, 82, 85-6, 95
Elasticity of demand 47
Emerging markets 69
Energy dependence 42
Environmental impact 64, 103, 114-15
Environmental protection 33
Equality 37
Ethical decisions 64-7
Ethical trading 108
Ethnocentric model 85
European Union 22-3, 59, 115
Euro 26-7, 111-12, 115
European Central Bank (ECB) 27
European Commission 24-5
Exchange rates 53, 59
Exploitation 66, 101, 105
Export-led growth 19, 31
Exports 113
Extension strategies 94
External costs 20-21

Fair Trade 65, 108
Financial crashes 2
Fiscal stimulus 34
Flexibility 71
Foreign aid 20
Foreign direct investment (FDI) 4, 19-20, 23, 30, 38, 96

Free trade 19
Free trade areas 22

G20 4
G8 4
Geocentric approach 86
Global brands 83-4, 86-7
Global localisation 79
Global marketing 85-8
Global sourcing 11-13
Globalisation 11, 13, 15, 19-21, 78
Glocalisation 86-8
Government grants 53, 95, 101-2, 104
Great Depression 2, 18
Green Revolution 36

Harmonisation 24, 79
Human capital 18, 55
Human Development Index (HDI) 51

Import controls 76
Import substitution 36
Imports, competing 7
Income distribution 29-30, 46
Income elasticity of demand 83
India 35-9
Inelastic demand 74, 90
Inequality 29, 113-14
Infant industries 76
Infrastructure 18, 39, 52
Innovation 7, 70, 80, 84, 97, 105
Inorganic growth 5, 80-2
Intellectual property rights (IPR) 52, 80, 97
Interdependence 4
Intermediate products 11
International Monetary Fund (IMF) 3, 76, 78
Investment 18, 37
Investment appraisal 51
Inward-looking policies 73, 76
Irrigation 39

Joint ventures 11-12, 20, 30, 46, 70-1

Keynes, J.M. 79

Labour, low-cost, 4, 10-12, 23, 55
Labour intensive production 64
Legal framework 43, 52
Level playing field 24
Long Tail 90

Market mapping 47-9
Market orientation 49
Market penetration 6-7
Market positioning 49
Market research 49, 70, 87
Market saturation 6, 45, 82, 94
Market segments 9, 46-9, 69, 83, 91
Market share 6-8, 82, 83
Marketing mix 85-6, 88
Mergers 80, 82
Monetary policy 111-13
Monopsony power 102
Multinational corporations (MNCs) 4, 20, 80, 92-9, 109-10
Multiplier 96, 98, 104

New product development 84
Newly industrialised economies (NIEs) 44
Niche markets 89
Non-tariff barriers 74
North American Free Trade Area (NAFTA) 4, 22

Office of Fair Trading 6-7
Offshoring 11
Open economy 31, 36
Opportunity cost 57, 59, 63
Organic growth 5, 80
Outsourcing 10-12, 15, 79
Outward looking economies 44

Political instability 52

Pressure groups 63, 106-7
Pricing strategies 69
Primary products 17
Process innovation 8
Product life cycle 8
Productive efficiency 25
Productivity 18-19, 37
Promotional message 86-8
Protection 73-5
Protectionism 74-7
Public sector deficits 111-12
Purchasing power parity 37

Qualitative market research 46
Quantitative data 46
Quotas (import) 72, 74

Rationalisation 82
Recession 18, 34
Recruitment 54
Research and development 7-8
Reverse innovation 88
Russia 42-43

Safety standards 75
Savings 37
Self-regulation 108
Shareholder value 62
Shocks 2
Short-termism 62
Single European market 19, 22-4, 26
Skill shortages 113
Social and cultural differences 68, 71, 86
Social audits 66
Social responsibilities – see corporate social responsibility
South Africa 44
Specialisation 4, 22, 56
Stakeholder approach 62-3
Standard of living 29
State-owned enterprises 32
Structural change 1-2, 20
Subcultures 89
Subsidies 39
Supply chain 10-11, 14, 38
Sustainability 64, 101
Sweatshops 101
Synergy 82

Takeovers/acquisitions 5, 80-2
Target markets 46, 48
Tariffs 24, 72-3
Tax avoidance 100-101, 113-14
Tax rates 53
Technical change 8, 13
Technology 18, 59
Technology transfer 31, 47, 97
Trade balance 98
Trade barriers – see barriers to trade
Trade blocs 4, 19
Trade creation 24-25
Trade diversion 24-25
Trade liberalisation 3, 13, 19, 79
Trade negotiations 76
Trade patterns 59
Trade surpluses 31, 111-12
Trade deficits 111-12
Trade unions 65
Trade-offs 63
Trading blocs 19, 22
Transfer pricing 100-101
Transport costs 14-15.

UN Climate Conference 67
Uncertainty 49, 53
Undervalued exchange rates 75
Unemployment 21, 34, 104
United Nations 2
Unsustainable growth 21, 103

Working conditions 64-5, 102
World Bank 3, 20, 76
World Trade Organisation (WTO) 3, 18, 76-7, 78